Joseph Haydn

Pauline D. Townsend

CAMBRIDGE UNIVERSITY PRESS

Cambridge, New York, Melbourne, Madrid, Cape Town,
Singapore, São Paolo, Delhi, Mexico City

Published in the United States of America by Cambridge University Press, New York

www.cambridge.org
Information on this title: www.cambridge.org/9781108064804

© in this compilation Cambridge University Press 2013

This edition first published 1884
This digitally printed version 2013

ISBN 978-1-108-06480-4 Paperback

This book reproduces the text of the original edition. The content and language reflect the beliefs, practices and terminology of their time, and have not been updated.

Cambridge University Press wishes to make clear that the book, unless originally published by Cambridge, is not being republished by, in association or collaboration with, or with the endorsement or approval of, the original publisher or its successors in title.

CAMBRIDGE LIBRARY COLLECTION
Books of enduring scholarly value

Music

The systematic academic study of music gave rise to works of description, analysis and criticism, by composers and performers, philosophers and anthropologists, historians and teachers, and by a new kind of scholar - the musicologist. This series makes available a range of significant works encompassing all aspects of the developing discipline.

Joseph Haydn

Admired and studied by both Mozart and Beethoven, Franz Joseph Haydn (1732–1809) imbued his life-enhancing compositions with wit, elegance and deep emotion. His output was prolific and included symphonies (most notably those written during his two visits to London, where he received a rapturous welcome), string quartets, chamber music, piano sonatas and choral works. This concise biography, first published in 1884, forms part of music critic Francis Hueffer's *Great Musicians* series, which was intended to provide succinct accounts of popular composers for the general reader. The author, Pauline D. Townsend, drew much of her material for the book from the painstaking research on Haydn published by the German musicologist Carl Ferdinand Pohl, archivist and librarian of the Vienna Society of the Friends of Music. A list of Haydn's works forms an appendix, based on the information in Grove's *Dictionary of Music and Musicians*.

Cambridge University Press has long been a pioneer in the reissuing of out-of-print titles from its own backlist, producing digital reprints of books that are still sought after by scholars and students but could not be reprinted economically using traditional technology. The Cambridge Library Collection extends this activity to a wider range of books which are still of importance to researchers and professionals, either for the source material they contain, or as landmarks in the history of their academic discipline.

Drawing from the world-renowned collections in the Cambridge University Library and other partner libraries, and guided by the advice of experts in each subject area, Cambridge University Press is using state-of-the-art scanning machines in its own Printing House to capture the content of each book selected for inclusion. The files are processed to give a consistently clear, crisp image, and the books finished to the high quality standard for which the Press is recognised around the world. The latest print-on-demand technology ensures that the books will remain available indefinitely, and that orders for single or multiple copies can quickly be supplied.

The Cambridge Library Collection brings back to life books of enduring scholarly value (including out-of-copyright works originally issued by other publishers) across a wide range of disciplines in the humanities and social sciences and in science and technology.

HAYDN.

The Great Musicians

Edited by FRANCIS HUEFFER

JOSEPH HAYDN

BY

PAULINE D. TOWNSEND

TRANSLATOR OF JAHN'S "MOZART"

LONDON

SAMPSON LOW, MARSTON, SEARLE, & RIVINGTON

CROWN BUILDINGS, 188, FLEET STREET

1884

[*All rights reserved*]

LONDON:
GILBERT AND RIVINGTON, LIMITED,
ST. JOHN'S SQUARE.

PREFACE.

GREAT musical learning and indefatigable ardour of research have enabled Herr C. F. Pohl (Librarian to the Gesellschaft der Musikfreunde, Vienna) to accomplish for Haydn what Spitta has done for Bach, Jahn for Mozart, and Chrysander for Handel. The two volumes of his " Joseph Haydn," already published (Leipzig, 1878 and 1882), bring the story of the composer's life down to the end of the year 1790, the date of his departure for England. The second part of the same writer's " Mozart und Haydn in London" (Vienna, 1867) continues the narrative to 1795, the close of Haydn's musical career.

The present writer desires to make full acknowledgment of her indebtedness to Herr Pohl's work, and at the same time to indicate, as her further principal authorities on all matters of fact contained in this volume, Haydn's Autobiographical Sketch written for " Das gelehrte Oesterreich " in 1776, and first published in the " Wiener Zeitschrift für Kunst, Literatur und Mode," in 1836; Griesinger's "Biographische Notizen über J. Haydn" (Leipzig, 1810); Dies's " Biographische Nachrichten von J. Haydn" (Vienna, 1810); von Karajan's " J. Haydn in

London, 1791 und 1792" (Vienna, 1861); Carpani's "Le Haydine" (2nd edit., 1823); the article on Haydn in Fitis's "Biographie Univ. des Musiciens;" and last, though not least, the article "J. Haydn," by Herr Pohl, in Grove's "Dictionary of Music and Musicians." The list of Haydn's compositions given at the end of the volume is mainly based upon that in Grove's dictionary.

CONTENTS.

CHAPTER I.
CHILDHOOD AND EARLY LIFE, 1732—1750—ROHRAU—HAINBURG—VIENNA 1

CHAPTER II.
STUDY IN VIENNA, 1750—1760 14

CHAPTER III.
CAPELLMEISTER AT EISENSTADT, 1760—1766 30

CHAPTER IV.
WORKS AT EISENSTADT, 1760—1766 47

CHAPTER V.
ESTERHAZ, 1766—1790 60

CHAPTER VI.
FIRST VISIT TO LONDON, 1790—1792 80

CHAPTER VII.
SECOND VISIT TO LONDON, 1794, 1795 102

CHAPTER VIII.

The "Creation"—The "Seasons"—Haydn's Last Years—
   Conclusion 111

List of Haydn's Compositions 121

HAYDN.

CHAPTER I.

CHILDHOOD AND EARLY LIFE, 1732—1750.

ROHRAU—HAINBURG—VIENNA.

THE interest of the life of Joseph Haydn centres almost exclusively in his career as a musician. As we trace his artistic progress step by step, we do not, as is the case with Mozart, come across pleasant side glimpses of home interiors, bright with the love of wife or sister and welcome to the observer as showing the man as he was in his best and truest moods. Nor do Haydn's letters which have been preserved possess much general or human interest, although they are valuable, as letters always must be, in helping us to form a true estimate of his character.

His disposition would seem to have fitted him admirably for a domestic life, but this blessing was denied him. His childhood ended at six years old, and from that time until he was sixty-five he had, properly speaking, no home nor home life. His life and his art were indissolubly bound together; his friendships, though the view we get of these is so pleasant and life-like as almost to contradict what we have been saying, were all with his fellow-artists or his patrons.

He cared for nothing, lived for nothing but music, and his sole regret in extreme old age was that he must die before having carried his art to greater perfection than it had yet attained. This being so, it behoves the biographer of Haydn to centre the interest of his life in the work of his life, and, while eagerly gathering such crumbs as he may find of information as to Haydn the man, to strive to give his readers a clear and accurate portrait of Haydn the musician. To do this, however, imperfectly, will be the aim of the present sketch, and it will involve a description of Haydn's surroundings, physical and human, and of the times in which he lived and worked, which, it is hoped, will supply that element of general interest which a mere record of dates, events, and compositions would certainly lack.

Haydn's birthplace was the little village of Rohrau, lying, as its name implies, in a flat, marshy district close to the River Leitha, which here forms the boundary between Lower Austria and Hungary, and later falls into a tributary of the Danube. The house in which the great composer first saw the light stands at the end of the long village street nearest to the Leitha and the bridge spanning the river, and was consequently at the mercy of the floods, which laid the low-lying country under water as often as the river overflowed its banks. Twice since the cottage was built by Haydn's father has it been swept away; first in 1813, and again in 1833. Twice has it been rebuilt, each time in its original form, so that the present single-storied, straggling little house, with its thatched roof and over-shadowing tree, may be accepted as a very faithful presentment of Haydn's earliest home.

The workshop in which Mathias Haydn, the father, carried on his trade as a wheelwright has disappeared, but the orchard and kitchen garden, stretching almost to the banks of the Leitha, are still to be seen, and here we may imagine Joseph, like any other sturdy little German peasant, passing the first six years of his life, playing, shouting, tumbling, and getting into all the mischief within his reach. Not only his father, but four or five of his six uncles also were wheelwrights by trade. The family came originally from Hainburg on the Danube, about four leagues from Rohrau. There most of Mathias Haydn's brothers still pursued their calling, and there also a connection by marriage named Frankh was schoolmaster and Chorregent.

Mathias Haydn may be described as a last-century German peasant of the best type. An honest, God-fearing, hard-working man, content with his own lot in life, but not without a spark of ambition for his sons; so that as his little Joseph's talent for music became more and more marked, he liked to imagine him a future Capellmeister or Chorregent. Ignorant enough, doubtless, he was of all outside his trade, but not absolutely uncultivated either, since during a visit to Frankfort in his youth, undertaken for some purpose connected with his trade, he had learned to play the harp by ear, and was fond of singing to its accompaniment, sometimes alone, sometimes in duets with his wife. As the children grew up they were allowed to join in these family concerts, and their father took pride in teaching them to sing in parts correctly. In after-years, when Joseph and his younger brother Michael, both studying music in Vienna, were spending their holidays at home, the evening music was resumed. One can imagine how eagerly the old man would produce his instrument and uplift his still pleasing tenor voice, as one who would say, "And I, too, am a musician!" Then the sons, with all the arrogance of youthful knowledge, would question this or that point in the father's rendering of voice part or accompaniment, and the dispute waxing warm, Mathias would finally close it with the angry and unanswerable remark, "You are a set of donkeys!"

Mathias Haydn married in 1728 Maria Koller, daughter of the "Marktrichter" and cook to Count Harrach, lord of the castle and village of Rohrau. She was a girl of twenty-one when her husband brought her home to his newly-built cottage, and here she bore him twelve children, and lived a faithful wife and mother till her death in 1754.

Joseph's love for his mother was deep and lasting, and, considering the early age at which he left her side never to return as an inmate of the home, this fact points to a more than ordinary maternal influence.

The habits of order, regularity, and hard work which

she inculcated, lasted to the end of his life, and to a visitor who expressed surprise at finding him when over seventy years of age fully dressed and with freshly powdered periwig on early in the morning, he gratefully declared that the strictness with which his mother had insisted on neatness and order in her children from the earliest youth had made these habits second nature to him.

Franz Joseph Haydn, known to the world as Joseph Haydn, the second child of this worthy couple, was born in 1732. The exact day of his birth is variously given as the 31st of March or the 1st of April. He himself held to the latter date, and declared that his brother Michael had invented the earlier, lest people should call him a born April fool! The probability is that his birth took place during the night between the last day of March and the first of April.

There is little to tell of Haydn's early childhood. It differed in no respect from that of the other village children with whom he played in the meadows, and went to and from the village school, sent there no doubt as soon as he could toddle to be safe out of the way of the busy mother and the younger babies, who followed each other into the world in rapid succession. The little fellow soon began to give signs of a good musical ear; his special treats were the evening duets of the father and mother, and one can imagine him perched on a stool in the corner of the low, dark living-room, listening with all his ears, and occasionally venturing to join in with a pretty childish treble. We may imagine him, too, loitering behind the other children when school was over, listening with open-eyed wonder to the performances upon the violin with which the village schoolmaster solaced his evening leisure. "That must be such easy music to make!" thinks little Joseph. "One has only to find two nice smooth pieces of wood and rub one of them gently up and down the other;" and, provided with his instrument, he set himself gravely by his father's side and joined in the evening concert, keeping strict time, and imitating the schoolmaster's handling of the bow to admiration.

The delighted father began to imagine a brilliant future for his eldest son. Who could tell that he might not, with industry and good luck, rise to be a Capellmeister, or at least Chorregent, like cousin Frankh at Hainburg? The mother had other and less worldly dreams, and would fain have seen the boy devoted to a priestly career. But Mathias's stronger will prevailed, and at Frankh's next visit to Rohrau, he was pressed to give his judgment on Joseph's voice and ear. With an eye to his own advantage as well as to his little cousin's future fame, he offered to take entire charge of him and begin his musical education without delay. The father's eager consent was given, the mother's hesitation overcome; solacing herself with the thought that as Chorregent or Capellmeister it would still be open to Joseph to enter the priesthood and fulfil her dearest wish, she began with all a mother's hopes and fears to prepare her little son for his early flight from the parent nest. Sepperl,[1] finding himself suddenly the centre of the family interest, betrayed little grief at parting, but listened dutifully to his mother's exhortations as to cleanliness and good behaviour; and when the morning of his departure arrived, having bid adieu to his friend the schoolmaster, and sought the blessing of the good priest of the village, he bravely mounted the waggon by his father's side, and made his first plunge into the wide world.

Early as he left his home, Haydn never forgot it, nor did the friendship and flattery of the great ever tempt him in after-years to feel ashamed of his lowly origin. On the contrary, he was proud of having, as he expressed it, "made something out of nothing;" and his poorer relations, of whom he had plenty, had no cause to complain of his want of generosity. The actual place of his birth was dear to him, and we are told by an eye-witness that in 1795, when he was making his triumphal return from his second visit to London, and was invited by Count Hàrrach to inspect the monument erected to his honour in the grounds of Castle Rohrau, Haydn stopped

[1] The Austrian diminutive for "Joseph."

short on the threshold of the little cottage that had been his home, and kneeling down, kissed the ground made sacred to him by the footsteps of his father and mother.

The short journey from Rohrau to Hainburg is an interesting one to the lover of antiquity or the student of history; the country around is thickly strewn with Roman remains, and the little town of Petronell, which lies about half-way between the two, covers the site of the Roman city Carnuntum, destroyed by Attila. A mile south of Petronell is the Heidenthor, the ruins of a triumphal arch erected by Augustus to commemorate the conquest of Pannonia by Tiberius.

Mathias Haydn and his little son, however, were little likely to feel any association with these relics of a past age, or to have an eye for anything but the first sight of the schoolhouse which was to be the end of their journey. The father's heart must have beat high with hopes and fears when the picturesque old town, with its walls and towers, came in sight, and his mind must have been full of the memories of his own early youth as the humble conveyance passed slowly through the Wienerthor, one of the two castellated gateways planted at the extremities of the principal street. Fifty-five years before, on July 11th, 1683, Hainburg had been stormed and pillaged by the Turks, and Haydn's great-great-grandfather had barely escaped with his life. Since then it had been rebuilt, and was now a flourishing market-town. The school, in which the elements of an ordinary education were given to the boys, together with special training as choristers, was, as we have seen, at that time under the direction of Johann Mathias Frankh, who united the offices of schoolmaster and Chorregent, and bore the title of Schulrector. He was a man of about thirty, possessed of considerable musical knowledge, and a severe, though by no means conscientious teacher. He was more than once called to account by the authorities for neglect of his duties as schoolmaster, and later on was dismissed (though afterwards reinstated in his office) on a charge of gambling with loaded dice. To Haydn he gave, as the latter declared, more blows than victuals; but he earned his gratitude as a teacher nevertheless, as is proved by a bequest in Haydn's will to the daughter of Frankh and her husband, Philipp Schimpel, at that time Chorregent, of 100 florins and a portrait of Frankh, "my first instructor in music."

It was on the side of Frankh's wife that the relationship with the Haydn family existed. She was Julie Rosine, daughter of Mathias Seefranz, who was the second husband of Haydn's grandmother. She seems to have neglected her duty towards the little fellow confided to her care, and the change to poor Joseph must have been great. He has recorded his distress at finding himself, for want of his mother's care, becoming "a dirty little urchin," and the fact of a child of six years old being compelled to wear a wig "for the sake of cleanliness," gives one a pathetic idea of his forlorn state. Haydn had, fortunately for himself and the world, a naturally buoyant and cheerful disposition, which sustained him under the petty oppressions and annoyances, which are the inevitable lot of a youth of genius struggling upward, and he seems even at this early age to have taken Frankh's cuffs and hard words, and his wife's neglect with all the philosophy possible to him. Dies relates the only musical anecdote of him which has come down to us from this time, and which reminds us of many such stories told of the young Mozart.

There was to be a great church festival, including a procession through the streets of the town, in which the choristers were, as a matter of course, to take part. But the drummer falling ill, no one could be found to take his place, till Frankh called for Joseph Haydn, showed him how to make the stroke, and left him to practise it alone. Joseph found a meal tub, stretched a cloth over the top, set it on a stool, and began to drum away with such vigour that the stool was soon overturned and himself covered with meal dust. But the stroke was learnt, and the spectators of the melancholy procession found their gravity unduly taxed by the sight of a little fellow of six years old beating a big drum, carried before him by a hunchback, as a bearer of ordinary stature would have raised the instrument far out of his reach. The drums on which he performed this feat are still preserved in the choir of the church at Hainburg.

Joseph had been two years at Hainburg, and was consequently between seven and eight years old, when an event occurred which marks the commencement of the second epoch of his musical career. Georg Reutter, Capellmeister of the Cathedral of St. Stephen in Vienna, passed through Hainburg in the course of a journey undertaken in search of boys' voices to recruit his choir. Hearing from Frankh of the musical talent of his little cousin, he singled him out from among the choristers summoned to sing before him, and, charmed by his "weak but pleasing voice" (as Haydn himself says), he sent for him to the house where he was staying. Placing a canon before the boy, he desired him to sing it at sight, and Haydn obeyed with so much readiness and correctness of ear that Reutter was delighted. He saw the little fellow as he sang cast longing glances at a plate of cherries on the table, and throwing a handful into his cap, he said, "Well done, you little rascal! Can you make a shake?"

"No," answered Sepperl, unabashed. "But no more can my cousin Frankh."

Reutter laughed at the ready answer, and taking Joseph between his knees he explained to him shortly how to take the intervals that compose a shake, and bade him try. The first attempt was sufficiently good to show that here was a pupil who would do honour to his teacher, and Reutter at once offered to take Haydn into the Cantorei of St. Stephen, and charge himself with his musical future. Provided the parents consented to this arrangement, Haydn was to remain at Hainburg until he had completed his eighth year, and then at once to proceed to Vienna. The consent of the parents, as may be supposed, was not difficult to obtain. The father saw his highest ambition on the way to be realized, and the mother, who still cherished secret hopes of the priesthood for Joseph, looked upon this step as one in the right direction. The boy himself was not too young to feel pride in his advancement, but he used to say afterwards that he never saw a plate of cherries without thinking of that day, and his first introduction to Capellmeister Reutter.

The Vienna of Haydn's day contained about a fifth of the number of its present inhabitants. The city has been variously compared to a ring with a centre of brilliants surrounded by a row of emeralds, and a further row of parti-coloured gems; and to a spider's web, the centre near St. Stephen's Cathedral, whence the streets radiate outwards in every direction and are encircled mid-way by a belt of boulevards called Ringe. This green belt (the emeralds of the ring) is laid out upon the ground that was the *Glacis* of the city until 1858, when the fortifications were destroyed. It forms the boundary of Vienna proper, and beyond it are the thirty-four suburbs (Vorstädte), stretching further into the country as the city increases year by year. In the centre and older quarter are all the principal churches, the palaces of the emperor and the nobility, the public offices, and the best shops. Here stands the Cathedral of St. Stephen, with its wonderful spire and beautiful doorways, and here—one of a row of small houses built close over against the principal doorway (Riesenthor)—was at that time the Cantorei, or choir school, where the next ten years of Haydn's life, the most important of his artistic career, were to be spent. The Cantorei of St. Stephen's was of very ancient foundation. It is mentioned in official documents as early as 1441, and the constitution of the school may be gathered from directions given concerning it in 1558—1571. It was newly constituted in 1663, and many alterations were made then and afterwards, but in its main points it was the same in Haydn's day as it had been for nearly a century before. The school consisted of a Cantor (made Capellmeister in 1663), a Subcantor, two ushers, and six scholars. The number had beer thirteen, but was reduced in 1715. They all lived together, and had meals in common. All expenses were paid by the town, and a fairly liberal allowance was made for the board, lodging, and clothing of the scholars.

But the cost of living had increased since this sum had been fixed, and the boys of Haydn's time were poorly fed and scantily clothed. They rejoiced greatly when they were summoned to sing at private banquets, for then they were sure of a good meal and a small present in money, which was always put into a box to form a common fund for the supply of any little luxuries granted to the boys.

The teachers had formerly been obliged to give instruction in music to the pupils of the neighbouring town schools, but this obligation had been removed, and their duties were now confined to the Cantorei. Here they taught their boys religion and Latin, together with the ordinary subjects of school education, and in music the violin, clavier, and singing. Singing must have been very carefully taught to enable the boys to perform as they did difficult masses and other church compositions at first sight. Haydn's musical instructors at St. Stephen's were Gegenbauer and Finsterbusch; little but their name is known of either, except that the former also taught the violin, and the latter had, according to Haydn, "a fine tenor voice." The more advanced scholars instructed the younger ones, and Joseph's delight was great when his younger brother Michael joined the choir and was placed under his care.

The labours of the choir might be considered severe. There were two full choral services daily in the cathedral, viz. High Mass and Vespers, with all their subdivisions; special *Te Deums* were constantly sung, and the singing boys had to take part in the numerous solemn processions of religious brotherhoods through the city, as well as in the thanksgiving services for the deliverance of Vienna from the siege of the Turks, for royal birthdays, and other such occasions. During Holy Week the labours of the choir were continuous. On Palm Sunday the archbishop and clergy went in solemn procession, carrying palms, while the choristers and priests sang alternate verses from the Gospel account of Christ's entry into Jerusalem, and the boys spread their church vestments on the floor of the cathedral. The Passion

Play formerly given in the cathedral on Good Friday, had been discontinued, and in its place there was now a procession bearing an image of Christ to be laid in a sepulchre prepared in one of the side chapels; on the following day a similar representation of the Resurrection took place. Children's processions were very frequent, and Haydn's delight in after-years at the performance of the charity children at St. Paul's, may have been partly owing to the reminiscences awakened by it of these early days.

All this, it will be seen, left very little time for the study of theory and composition, even if Reutter (or Von Reutter after 1740, when he was ennobled) had felt any conscientious desire to make thorough musicians of the boys. Haydn could not remember having more than two lessons in composition from him, but this very neglect, which would have been fatal to any but a fine genius, stimulated the boy's ardour by throwing him back upon his own resources, and forcing him to exert his powers of originality and invention.

Music became his passion. Fond as he was of play and fun, he would leave his companions in the midst of the most enticing game whenever St. Stephen's organ sounded from within the cathedral, and he tried to play every instrument that he could lay his hands on. At thirteen the ardour of composition seized him, and sheet after sheet was covered with notes, "the fuller the better," till at length Reutter, finding him hard at work at a mass in thirteen parts, asked him scornfully if he had not better make two serve his purpose as a beginning, and learn to write music before he began to compose it. Undaunted, Joseph took the hint. Debarred from verbal instruction, he sought the aid of such books as he could obtain. An appeal for money to his father brought six florins from the worthy Mathias, which were speedily laid out on Fux's "Gradus ad Parnassum," and Mattheson's "Vollkommener Capellmeister." These books, especially the former, became Joseph's constant study. "The talent was in me," he says, "and by dint of hard work I managed to get on." He was fond of recalling in his old age these days of study and self-improvement. In 1808, a year before his death, having come to Vienna for some church festival, the boys of the Cantorei were brought before him, introduced by Hummel and Haydn's favourite pupil, Anton Polzelli. The old man looked kindly at the boys, and addressed them in the words : " I was once a singing boy. Reutter brought me from Hainburg to Vienna. I was industrious when my companions were at play ; I used to take my little clavier under my arm, and go off to practise undisturbed. When I sang a solo, the baker near St. Stephen's yonder always gave me a cake as a present. Be good and industrious, and serve God continually."

Haydn's musical zeal, however, did not prevent occasional outbursts of fun and mischief. On one occasion, the boys of the Cantorei having been sent for to sing at Schönbrunn, where the court was then residing, enjoyed the fuller liberty of the palace gardens, after their close quarters at St. Stephen's. The Empress Maria Theresa was then completing the building of the palace begun by Leopold I., and the workmen's scaffolding presented an overpowering temptation to the boys, who were soon astride on the beams as high up as they dared to climb. Prohibitions were of little avail, and the ringleader and most adventurous of the band, pointed out to Capellmeister Reutter by the empress herself, proved to be none other than Joseph Haydn. " Give him a good hiding," was the imperial command, forthwith executed ; and in after-years, Haydn took an opportunity of thanking the empress for this her first proof of royal favour.

Haydn's progress and performances were so creditable to the Cantorei that Reutter had no hesitation in making an offer to Mathias Haydn of the same advantages for his younger son Michael, who accordingly joined his brother at St. Stephen's to their mutual delight. His advent, however, was destined to cut short Joseph's career as a chorister. His voice was stronger and of better quality than Joseph's, which was about breaking ; and on one occasion the empress, declaring that " Joseph Haydn sang like a crow," desired that Michael might take his place. Michael accordingly sang a *Salve Regina* with such sweetness and pathos, that Maria Theresa sent for him and rewarded him with twenty-four ducats. When Reutter asked him what he meant to do with so much money, he promptly answered, "I shall send half to my father, and keep the other half till my voice breaks." Reutter applauded so prudent a resolution, and offered to take charge of the twelve ducats himself; but he seems to have forgotten to produce them when the appointed time came.

Henceforth Reutter was only upon the watch for an excuse for discharging Joseph, now in his eighteenth year. A boyish freak, showing the somewhat thoughtless love of fun which distinguished him through life, gave the desired opportunity. The possession of a new pair of scissors tempted Joseph to try their quality on every object that came within his reach. A schoolfellow's pigtail hung temptingly before him; snap went the scissors, down fell the pigtail, and the decree went forth from the Capellmeister that for this offence Joseph Haydn must be caned on the palm of his hand. Furious at the proposed indignity, Joseph declared that he would leave the Capellhaus rather than submit to it. "So you shall," said Reutter, "but you shall be caned first, and then off with you, as soon as you like!" And so it befell that Joseph Haydn found himself in the streets of Vienna on a November evening of the year 1749, penniless, homeless, and with no future prospects whatever.

CHAPTER II.

STUDY IN VIENNA.

1750—1760.

THE turning-point in Haydn's career thus reached, it will be well, before entering upon the struggles, privations, and earnest labours of his early manhood, to gain a clear idea, however slight may be the sketch which affords it, of the stage on which the second act of his life's drama was to be played. The Vienna of the second half of the eighteenth century was the capital of the most ancient and glorious, if not still the most powerful empire of Europe, inhabited by a proud and wealthy nobility, a prosperous middle-class, and a silent, if not a contented, lower class.

Vienna was essentially a city of pleasure. That brilliant display of intellect and wit which was to be found in the *salons* of Paris before the Revolution, was wanting in the palaces of the Viennese nobility; the presence of the court, and the prudent policy of the House of Austria, excluded all subjects of interest which might result in calling into question the divine right and supremacy of "the powers that be." Sensual pleasures alone remained to gratify the taste and kindle the emotions of society, and the natural result was a general lowering of the moral tone, and an absolute dearth of high aims or noble achievements either in individuals or the community at large.

A sort of artificial stimulus to the cultivation of science and art was given by the Emperor Joseph II., the son and successor of Maria Theresa. Himself a man of considerable refinement and even learning, he founded

several valuable scientific institutions, and liberally patronized the arts, especially music, the taste for which was hereditary in his family. Following the example of the court, the great nobles vied with each other in maintaining expensive musical establishments; but that the Viennese generally were not enthusiastic for art, the following description of them, written in 1768 by that shrewd observer, Leopold Mozart, will sufficiently show:—
"The Viennese public, as a whole, has no love of anything serious or sensible, they cannot even understand it, and their theatres furnish abundant proof that nothing but utter trash, such as dances, burlesques, harlequinades, ghost tricks, and devil's antics will go down with them. You may see a fine gentleman, even with an order on his breast, laughing till the tears run down his face, and applauding with all his might some piece of senseless buffoonery; whilst in a most pathetic scene, where the situation and action are alike irresistibly fine and pathetic, and where the dialogue is of the highest order, he will chatter so loud with a lady that his better informed neighbours can scarcely hear a word of the play."

Music was an exotic imported from Italy, not of home growth; it was the art of the court, not of the people, and its fortunes rose and fell with the fortunes and caprices of the court. All musical compositions, great or small, were commanded either by the court or the nobility, or composed in the hope of gaining royal or noble patronage. The two theatres of Vienna proper, the Burg or Palace Theatre, and the Kärnthnerthor Theatre, were both under imperial control, and the strong predilection of the imperial family for Italian music caused the failure of all attempts to introduce German opera or German singers. Even so late as 1785, when, the Kärnthnerthor Theatre being freed from its connection with the court, it was decided to place German opera there in competition with Italian opera, the want of national life and feeling again produced failure, as the following characteristic outburst from Mozart, disappointed at the short career of his "Entführung," will show:—

"I can give you" (he writes to the librettist Klein) "no present information as to the intended German opera, as (with the exception of the alterations at the Kärnthnerthortheater) everything goes on very quietly. It is to be opened at the beginning of October. I do not prophesy a very successful result. It seems to me that the plans now formed are more likely to end in the final overthrow of the temporarily depressed German opera than in its elevation and support. My sister-in-law, Lange, alone is to be allowed to join the German company. Cavalieri, Adamberger, Teyber, all pure Germans, of whom our fatherland may be proud, are to stay in the Italian theatre to oppose and rival their own countrymen. German singers at present may be easily counted! And even if they be as good as those I have named, which I very much doubt, the present management appears to me too economical and too little patriotic to think of paying the services of strangers, when they can have as good or better on the spot. The Italian *troupe* has no need of them in point of numbers; it can stand alone. ..... If only a single patriot were to come to the fore, it would give the affair another aspect. But in that case, perhaps, the budding national theatre would break forth into blossom; and what a disgrace it would be to Germany if we Germans once began in earnest to think, or act, or speak, or even—to *sing* German. Do not blame me, my dear sir, if I go too far in my zeal. Convinced that I am addressing a fellow-*German*, I give my tongue free course, which unfortunately is so seldom possible, that after such an outpouring of the heart one feels that he might get drunk without any risk of injuring his health."

In church music Germany was destined to triumph in the end, although its rules and forms were determined by the Neapolitan school, and at the time of which we are speaking church music was composed of much the same materials as Italian operatic music, and exercised much the same effect. This does not, of course, imply that operatic forms were directly imported into church music, which must necessarily be subordinate to the liturgical forms of Divine service; but the character of the music, its moral and artistic elements, became more and more secular, as the art strove to free itself from the fetters of tradition; the sway of the singer too was as mighty in the church as elsewhere, and demanded as many opportunities for display; and the idea that the worship of the Almighty was best promoted by satisfying the prevailing taste was united to the pleasure afforded by the actual performance of a first-rate vocalist.

Instrumental music, as a distinct branch of the art, and apart from the voice, was still in its infancy. We shall trace its progress as identified with that of Haydn himself, and we shall see how his genius succeeded in combining the natural strength and youthful freshness of musical Germany with the refinement, ease, and grace of the more matured art of Italy.

There was, however, one point at which the art of music and the daily life of the Viennese came into direct contact with each other. No amusement was so completely to the taste of the gay and laughter-loving public as that of dancing, and during the latter half of the eighteenth century it became an absolute rage. Dance music, at first minuets and "allemands" only, later on country dances, ländler and waltzes, developed into an important branch of composition, and the suite, consisting of a succession of dances in the same key, but differing in time, measure, and expression, no doubt suggested the division of the modern symphony and sonata form into separate movements, and also the direct importation of the minuet into serious orchestral compositions. The popular and individual character which Haydn took pains to give to his minuet movements proves that he considered the composition of dance music as such in no way derogatory to his dignity as a musician, and we are told that Mozart's official duties as Chamber Composer to the Emperor were limited to the production of dance music for the masked balls in the Imperial Redoutensäle.

After the erection of the Burg or Palace Theatre in 1752, the old Hof Theatre was converted into the large and small Redoutensäle now existing, and concerts, balls, &c.,

were given there. The balls were masked, and took place on every Carnival Sunday, or Shrove Tuesday, and on the three last days of Carnival. Joseph II. favoured them as a means of drawing classes together, and frequently appeared at them with his court. All classes mixed freely, and considerable licence was allowed. The usual dances were minuets, country dances, and waltzes, from the last of which the higher classes held aloof on account of the crowding (just as is the case in " Don Giovanni"). The management of the Redoute was generally in the same hands as that of the Opera Theatre, the two being farmed out together. The court monopolized both the Opera Theatre and the Kärnthnerthor Theatre, and kept the control over them until 1794. Thus it came about that the court theatrical director ordered the dance music, and although the pay was only a few ducats for a set of dances, the services of good composers were claimed for the purpose; Haydn, Gyrowetz, Hummel, Mozart, and Beethoven all composed for the Redoute. Well might Mozart write bitterly after the customary entry on the official return of his income as Court Composer,—"Too much for what I do; too little for what I could do."[1]

Haydn's reflections as he turned penniless, and with no clothes but those on his back, from the house which had been all that he had for home for the last ten years, must have been gloomy and hopeless enough to depress even his cheerful spirit. He could see little prospect of being able to support himself until by dint of hard study and many failures he could succeed in showing the talent that was "in him" by the composition of a work original and important enough to gain him the post of Capellmeister, which was the object of his ambition. As an instrumentalist he had neither hope nor intention of doing more than master some instrument sufficiently to gain a partial livelihood by teaching during his years of study; it was as a composer that he felt himself destined to succeed, and his confidence in his own powers urged him to waste

[1] Jahn's Life of Mozart (Eng. Edit.), vol. ii. p. 276

no time in empty regrets, but at once to adapt his life to the end which he had in view. This feeling prevented his seeking a refuge with his parents, which otherwise might have been the most natural course for him to take. His mother had never ceased importuning him to enter the Church, and this he had firmly resolved not to do; it would scarcely have been possible for him to burden his parents with his maintenance, and refuse to embrace so ready a means of becoming independent. Home, therefore, Joseph could not go. Those friends that he had in Vienna were little if any better off than himself; but they were all musical or connected with music, and if he could but find a temporary home with one of them, he might with industry and good fortune soon earn enough to supply his frugal needs and enable him to pursue his studies. Life at the Cantorei had taught him to limit his desires to the barest necessaries, and a life of privation and hardship would be no novelty to him.

It was on a November evening of the year 1749 that Haydn was dismissed the Cantorei, and the following morning found him still wandering through the streets of Vienna, worn out with hunger and fatigue. In this plight he fell in with an acquaintance named Spangler, a tenor singer at the Church of St. Michael, who, taking natural pity on the desolate condition of the youth, offered him shelter in the garret which he inhabited with his wife and child. Here Joseph remained through the rest of the winter, cold and hunger his constant companions, music his only and unfailing comfort. And though nature would now and then assert her sway, and sheer hunger drive him to doubt whether he would not do better to find some certain way of earning enough at all events to give him bread to eat, his buoyant spirit soon rose above the temptation, and his face was steadily set again towards a musical career. But Spangler's hospitality could not last for ever, nor was real and continued study possible in such close quarters. Haydn got through the winter as best he could, earning a scanty living by playing the violin at balls and elsewhere, by arranging compositions for one or more instruments, and by giving lessons for a trifling sum. With the return of spring his hopes rose, and numerous projects for the future flitted through his brain. One of these, impelled by hunger, he put into actual execution. Joining a party of pilgrims to the shrine of the Virgin at Mariazell, he presented himself to the choir-master as a former pupil at St. Stephen's, and showed some of his own attempts at sacred music as proofs of his fitness for admission into the choir. The choir-master roughly dismissed him, saying that he had lazy rascals enough from Vienna and wanted no more, whereupon Haydn mingled unperceived with the choir, and having vainly endeavoured to persuade the solo-singer to let him take his part, suddenly snatched the music out of the astonished youth's hand, and sang the solo in so finished a style that all the choir held their breath to listen. The choir-master sent for Joseph after the service, to apologize for his rude dismissal and invite him to remain at Mariazell over the day. The invitation was extended to a week, and Haydn returned to Vienna strengthened with food, and possessed of a small sum of money collected among the choir to supply his immediate needs.

It was not long after this adventure that an event occurred which placed Haydn above the pressure of actual want, and enabled him to devote himself to the study for which he longed so ardently. A good tradesman of Vienna, named Buchholz, out of sheer Christian charity, and perhaps with faith in the young man's future, lent him unconditionally 150 florins. An extract from Haydn's first will (dated 1801) will show how opportune was the favour, and how gratefully remembered : " To the Jungfrau Anna Buchholz 100 florins, in remembrance that in my youth and extreme need her grandfather made me a loan of 150 florins without interest, which I faithfully repaid fifty years ago."

Who now so happy as Joseph Haydn ? The first step in his fortunes was made, and henceforward his progress, though slow, was steady and assured. In possession of what must have seemed to his inexperience inexhaustible wealth, his first care was to secure a habitable chamber; this he found in the old "Michaelerhaus," formerly attached to a religious foundation, and at that time let out in tenements. The room of which Haydn took possession with much delight was a garret, partitioned off from a larger room, with scarcely space to turn round in, and hardly any light. It contained no stove, and the roof was in such bad repair that the rain and snow made unceremonious entry, and drenched the young artist in his bed. In winter the water in his jug froze so hard during the night, that he had to go and draw direct from the well. His immediate neighbours, successively a journeyman printer, a "Kammerheizer" (a functionary whose business it was to make up the fires in the apartments of a prince or nobleman), a footman, and a cook, were not of a class to respect his desire for quiet study; but none of these drawbacks succeeded in damping the ardour of aspiring genius, and with his little worm-eaten clavier as a constant companion Haydn was, as he himself expressed it, "too happy to envy the lot of kings." Fortune favoured while she frowned on him; for in bringing him to the Michaelerhaus she had placed him within reach of the two people who perhaps in all Vienna were most calculated to further his career as a musician. On the third story dwelt the renowned Italian poet Metastasio, who could not fail to take notice of the youth's ardour and genuine talent, and who later entrusted to Haydn the musical instruction of his favourite pupil, Marianne Martinez. He conferred on him a still greater benefit by introducing him to Porpora, the most eminent teacher of singing and composition of the day. But this was not yet. For eighteen long months Haydn lived and worked alone, supporting himself by giving lessons for a trifling payment, and by playing the violin in orchestras, and the organ in churches or private chapels when he could. Every spare moment was devoted to study and composition and his clavier. His Mattheson and his Fux were his only friends until one lucky day that he found himself with savings sufficient to enable him to invest in a new musical work. He selected, from the small stock submitted to him, the six first sonatas of C. Ph. Emanuel Bach, and the choice exercised an important influence on his future studies. He says himself, "I did not leave the clavier until I had mastered them all, and those who know me well must be aware that I owe very much to Emanuel Bach, whose works I understand and have thoroughly studied. Emanuel Bach himself once complimented me on this fact."[2]

It was the case, that as soon as Haydn's works began to be publicly known, Bach hailed him with delight as a disciple, and took occasion to send him word that "he alone had thoroughly understood his works and made a proper use of them." A later theoretical work of Emanuel Bach's, the "Treatise on the Right Method of playing the Clavier," soon after fell into Haydn's hands, and strengthened the impression made by the sonatas. The spirit of the work may be summed up in a very few words by Bach himself: "A musician cannot move others unless he be first moved himself." And again: "It seems to me that the first object of music is to touch the heart, and this can never be done by mere thumping, flourishing, and arpeggio-ing." Bach declared that the chief and best quality of music was melody, and he advised clavier-players to hear as much good singing as possible: "It gives the habit of thinking in song, and it is always well to sing a new idea aloud to oneself, so as to catch the right delivery." How strong an influence such teaching as this must have exercised on an ardent young spirit striving to free itself from the swathing-bands of tradition and ecclesiastical authority can be readily imagined, and it is pleasant to find Haydn at the end of his long life acknowledging his constant obligation to Emanuel Bach,[3] and Bach indignantly repudiating the calumny which accused them of jealousy and meanness in their professional dealings with each other.[4]

Haydn's devotion to his clavier was not so exclusive as to cause him to neglect his study of the violin, and the

[2] Griesinger, Biog. Notizen über J. Haydn, p. 13.
[3] Dies. Biogr. Nachr. von J. Haydn, p. 38.
[4] Pohl, Joseph Haydn, p. 138.

STUDY IN VIENNA. 23

" celebrated virtuoso " who was his instructor on the instrument can have been no other than Dittersdorf, with whom he now formed an acquaintance destined to ripen into close and intimate friendship. It is likely that Haydn's superior knowledge of composition enabled him to return Dittersdorf benefits in kind. To the world Dittersdorf is known chiefly as an instrumental and operatic composer; his popularity in Vienna was at one time enormous, but it fell with the fall of German opera, and he died in poverty and neglect. Haydn and Dittersdorf had many a merry prank together during these years of struggling poverty. One evening, at a time when Haydn's works were just beginning to be popular, as the friends were strolling down one of the narrow streets of Vienna, they heard the strains of a fiddle proceeding from a little beer-cellar. Haydn entering, asked the performer in a scornful tone, " Whose minuet is that you are playing ? " " Haydn's," answered the fiddle-player triumphantly. " It's a d—d bad minuet," replied Haydn drily, whereupon the enraged musician turned upon him, and would have broken his head with the fiddle had not Dittersdorf dragged him laughing away.

A favourite form of instrumental music in Vienna during the last century was the Serenata (or Nachtmusik), performed by night under the window of the person in whose honour it was composed. It did not consist, as in Italy and Spain, in a mere accompaniment to the voice of a guitar or a mandoline; solos, quartets, and choruses, sometimes accompanied by wind instruments alone, sometimes by a full orchestra, were performed, and great composers were fond of thus doing honour to their patrons and friends. Younger artists found this also a convenient way of securing an audience for their works, and it was perhaps with some such view that we find Haydn one evening during the autumn of 1751 directing the performance of a quintet of his own composition under the windows of Frau Franziska Kurz, the pretty wife of the favourite comedian and theatrical manager, Joseph Kurz. Kurz was too wide awake and experienced an *entrepreneur* not to come to the immediate conclusion that a man who could write music so full of life and spirit as this might be useful to him; he called Haydn into the house, and setting him down to the clavier bade him show his skill. The test chosen to put the young artist to was somewhat extraordinary. Extending himself at full length on two chairs, Kurz imitated the motions of a swimmer in distress, and desired Haydn, with this assistance to his imagination, to give a musical representation of a storm at sea. Haydn, who had never even seen the sea, could only shake his head and stare in blank amazement. At last, as Kurz began to grow impatient, he sat down in despair, and almost involuntarily fell into the measure which Kurz had intended to suggest. The comedian springing up embraced him, and declared that he and no other should compose the music to his new comic opera "Der neue krumme Teufel."

The subject thus given to Haydn for his first essay in dramatic composition was originated by the French poet Le Sage in his novel "Le Diable boiteux," and has been a favourite one with play-writers almost up to the present day. It details the love adventures of a Spanish student, and the assistance therein afforded him by the Prince of Darkness. It is the less necessary to enter upon any analysis of the work here, since Haydn's music to it has entirely disappeared, nor does it seem that Kurz ever employed him again, for which indeed posterity may be thankful, for who would have heard of Haydn had fate doomed him to the career of a composer of comic operas? For his share in the work he received twenty-four ducats, which he no doubt considered very ample payment.

It is not unlikely that it was the performance of this work which first drew the attention of Metastasio to the young musician living under the same roof with himself, and induced him to engage Haydn as music-master to his own favourite pupil, Marianne Martinez.

Metastasio had begun his career as a dramatic poet in Italy; his "Didone Abandonnata" was published at

Naples in 1724, and laid the foundation of his fame. In 1730 he went to Vienna as court poet to the Emperor Charles VI., and from that time until his death his fame as a librettist and writer of songs was unrivalled. He was a man of deep sensibility and exquisite taste; he had a passionate love of music, and said himself that he never wrote a song without composing it according to his own conception of its character.

Metastasio took up his residence in Vienna with Nicolai Martinez, Master of the Ceremonies to the Apostolic Nuncio. He became the intimate friend of the family, and carefully superintended the education of the children. Marianne (born about 1740) was his special favourite, and he instructed her in the Italian, French, and English languages. She possessed considerable musical talent, which afterwards made her house a favourite resort of many distinguished musicians. Mozart was very intimate with her, and they used to play duets of her composition at her musical receptions.

Haydn was engaged to give Marianne daily lessons on the clavier, and for this he was boarded free for three years, a more important result being his introduction to Porpora, from whom Marianne received singing-lessons. Haydn went with her to Porpora's house to play her accompaniments, and in return for his services the gruff old Maestro threw at him a certain amount of instruction in composition which Haydn only too gratefully picked up and treasured until he could turn it to good account. He even condescended to act as valet to Porpora, blacking his boots, and brushing his clothes, and putting up with many hard words in return for the instruction which was so valuable to him.

Porpora's fame has come down to the present day chiefly as a teacher of singing, in which department of his art he has probably had no equal, before or since; but he himself aspired to be remembered by his compositions, and his restless ambition would not suffer him to be content with the less brilliant lot in which consisted his true usefulness.

At the time when Haydn became acquainted with him he was giving lessons to the mistress of the Venetian Ambassador Correr. Here again Haydn's services as accompanist were required, and were in fact found so valuable, that when Correr with all his establishment, including the lady and her music-master, migrated to the favourite baths of Mannersdorf for the summer, Joseph must needs go too.

Mannersdorf is a charming spot, surrounded by woods which are the favourite haunt of the nightingale. Haydn, who always found his inspiration in the quiet and retirement of a country life, enjoyed the release from his comfortless garret and the dingy streets of the city with all the strength of his nature-loving heart. Here, too, he became acquainted with Gluck, Bonno, Wagenseil, and other musicians, and was intimately associated with them in the musical *soirées* which were the evening entertainment of the noble visitors to Mannersdorf. For his services as accompanist he received six ducats a month and his board at the servants' table.

Returned to Vienna, Haydn devoted himself with fresh ardour to his studies, of which we know little except that they were entirely without external help or guidance. No genius was ever more emphatically self-taught than Haydn. Thrown back upon his own resources, it was only, as he said, the talent that was in him, and his indomitable industry, that made him what he afterwards became. Long after his fame was firmly established, he devoted sixteen to eighteen hours a day to steady work, conscious that further progress in his art was always attainable. As time went on, he made friends who were not long in recognizing his talent, and auguring well for his future. Among these was Baron von Furnberg, a great lover of music, who possessed a country seat a short distance from Vienna, and invited Haydn to take the direction of his musical parties there. For this nobleman Haydn wrote several string trios, six scherzandi for wind instruments, the precursors of his symphonies, and what is more important, his first quartets (Trautwein, Nos. 58-75), for performance by the priest of the village, the steward, Haydn himself, and the violoncellist Albrechtsberger. These compositions bear the impress of the pleasanter lines upon which the young artist's life had fallen. Although not wanting in earnestness and occasional depth of thought, they are chiefly distinguished by their cheerful light-hearted tone, at times approaching actual jollity. Their originality won them speedy recognition as the work of a man of genius, as well as a fair share of the disapprobation and gloomy forebodings of the decay of an art so treated, which originality is sure to incur.

Haydn was now (1756-59) so much in request as a music-master in Vienna, that he was able to raise his terms, and on the strength of his improved income to move to a more comfortable lodging. It was soon after this that he became acquainted with the accomplished and noble-minded Countess von Thun, who, meeting with some of his compositions, expressed a desire to know their author. Hearing this, Haydn presented himself before the countess; she, seeing before her a young man shabbily clothed, and somewhat uncouth in manner, suspected an imposition, and questioned Haydn closely as to whether he were indeed the composer of the works she admired. His natural and touching account of his early life and struggle with poverty convinced and interested her, and she became from that time forth his warm friend and supporter. Her influence was doubtless joined to that of Fürnberg to procure for Haydn the post which, in 1759, put an end for ever to his struggles for daily bread. In the winter of this year he was appointed Capellmeister to Count Morzin, a Bohemian nobleman of great wealth and a passionate lover of music. It would seem that in Haydn's time the musical establishment (which the prince kept at his country house at Lukavec, near Pilsen) did not exceed sixteen or eighteen performers, occasionally strengthened by members of his household and servants. For this orchestra Haydn wrote several Divertimenti for wind and strings, various occasional compositions, and his first symphony in D, a work which, small and light as it is, betrays the hand of the master in its clearness of expression and unity of design.

During his winter residence in Vienna, Haydn was enabled to add to his income as Capellmeister by giving lessons. Being now twenty-eight years of age, and of a somewhat susceptible nature, it was little wonder that he should fall in love with one of his pupils, the younger daughter of a hairdresser named Keller. According to some of his biographers he had known the family for long, and had even lodged in the house.[5] So far, however, from finding his passion returned, Joseph learnt to his sorrow that the object of it was bent upon entering a cloister. She carried out her design, and the father, unwilling to lose the prospect of securing a rising musician as a son-in-law, persuaded Joseph to console himself with his elder daughter, Maria Anna.

In no particular is the laxity of morals among the Viennese of that day more apparent than in the lightness with which the marriage tie was regarded. Marriage seems to have been looked upon as a mere matter of convenience, and those who found no happiness in such unions thought themselves entitled to seek for pleasure and distraction elsewhere. Of love between Haydn and his wife there was never any question, but it is not probable that he knew beforehand that he was marrying a shrew. The whole picture of his married life is a lamentable one. A childless union where there is no love is the veriest purgatory upon earth; and while it is impossible to acquit Haydn of blame in his after-relations with his wife and other women, we may at least surmise that so easy-natured and amiable a man would have made the happiness of a wife who understood his character and appreciated his genius. Maria Anna did neither; as Haydn once said, "It was all the same to her whether he were an artist or a cobbler," and it was fortunate perhaps for them both, it was certainly fortunate for the world, that circumstances prevented their living together during great part of their married life. They were not formally separated until after Haydn's return from London in

[5] Dies, p. 43.

1792. Frau Haydn spent the last years of her life at Baden, near Vienna, and died there March 20th, 1800.

Haydn's good mother did not live to mourn over her eldest son's hasty and ill-considered marriage, nor to rejoice in the opening for him of a career more brilliant than she could have conceived in her most sanguine dreams. She died Feb. 23rd, 1754, in her forty-sixth year, and her husband married again in the following year. Five children were the fruit of this union, who all died in infancy. After the death of Mathias Haydn, his second wife married again, and seems to have been altogether lost sight of by her stepson, who, however, bequeathed her a small sum in his first will, "to be transferred to her children should she be no longer alive."

Soon after Haydn's marriage Count Morzin found himself obliged to curtail his expenses by discharging his musical establishment; not, however, without interesting himself to find a fresh post for his favourite Haydn. Fortunately for the latter, Prince Paul Anton Esterhazy had already been struck by the originality and youthful vigour of some compositions that he had heard while on a visit to Count Morzin. It was not difficult, therefore, to induce him to engage Haydn as second Capellmeister, and with this appointment Haydn's "Wanderjahre" came for ever to an end, his "Meisterjahre" began.

CHAPTER III.

CAPELLMEISTER AT EISENSTADT.

1760—1766.

No country in Europe could boast a nobility more ancient and wealthy than that of Hungary in the eighteenth century. The position of the country, forming, as it did, the bulwark of Christendom against the Turks, had given it an importance out of proportion to its size and political progress, and had served to foster and maintain the power of the warlike nobles and the principles of the feudal system longer in Hungary than elsewhere. The burghers and peasants looked to their lords for protection from their infidel and cruel foe, while the lords exacted from them in return all the submission and substantial support of subjects to a sovereign. The close of the Thirty Years' War, and the final repulse of the Turks at the close of the seventeenth century, had left men weary of strife and bloodshed, and eager to turn to the arts and pleasures of the peace to which they had so long been strangers. The great nobles of the empire requiring, as it were, a fresh *raison d'être* for their supremacy, vied with each other in the grandeur of their palaces and establishments, and justified their pretensions by the magnificence of their patronage.

The example of the imperial family turned the tide of fashion more particularly in the direction of the art of music, and, as we have already seen, no nobleman considered his establishment complete without a body of performers, vocal and instrumental, as large as his means would allow, headed by a musician more or less distinguished as Capellmeister.

Among the Hungarian nobility no family could boast an earlier origin, or a more unbroken series of valiant and distinguished heads than that of Esterhazy, and there was no other, perhaps, that had evinced so genuine and enlightened a preference for music apart from the love of display and pre-eminence. The founder of the princely line of the house of Esterhazy was Paul, son of the first Count Nicholas. He was born in 1635, and was raised to the dignity of a Prince of the Holy Roman Empire by Leopold I., in consideration of his military services. The latter part of his life was devoted to science and art, especially music, and to the construction of the magnificent palace of Eisenstadt, interesting to us mainly as the scene of the most fruitful years of Haydn's musical career. The palace, which was erected on a scale of unprecedented magnificence, contains, besides two hundred chambers for guests, a large hall adorned with frescoes, which in Haydn's time was used as a theatre and for the performances of the full orchestra; the ordinary daily music was given in a smaller room. The park, lying partly on the slope of the Leitha hills, and overlooking the plain, is beautiful and of great extent, and the gardens, hot-houses, and conservatories are among the finest in Europe. Five or six miles south of Eisenstadt is the fortress castle of Forchtenstein, given to Count Nicholas by Ferdinand II. in 1622, built on a steep rock of limestone 600 feet high, and containing many memorials of the long struggle with the Turks, notably a cistern 450 feet deep, hewn in the solid rock by Turkish prisoners of war. The family treasures used to be deposited at Forchtenstein, and an old family statute compelled every head of the house of Esterhazy to add to this treasure, and forbade his touching any part of it, except to redeem an Esterhazy from slavery.

Prince Paul died in 1713. His son, Joseph Anton, acquired enormous wealth, raising the Esterhazy family to the height of its glory. He left two sons, the elder of whom, Paul Anton, was reigning prince at the time that Haydn was discharged by Count Morzin. He it was, therefore, who, admiring the originality and vigour of one of Haydn's compositions which was performed before him, consented to engage the young composer as Vice-Capellmeister, a promise apparently forgotten as soon as made. As months went by, and no summons arrived for Haydn to enter upon his new duties, his friend Friedberg, the leader of the prince's orchestra, advised him to write a new symphony, and managed to have it performed on the birthday of the prince. This sufficed to call Haydn to remembrance, and his appointment was duly signed and ratified on May 1st, 1761.

No better way can, we venture to think, be found of giving to English readers a clear idea of the duties and position of a Capellmeister in the last century, and the relation in which the musical establishment of a great noble stood to himself and to the outside world, than by presenting verbatim the text of the agreement between Haydn and Prince Paul Anton. Our indignation is roused at finding a great artist placed in the position of an upper servant, and required to perform duties almost menial in their nature; while at the same time it cannot be denied that the obligation to continued and varied productive efforts, and the freedom from all immediate care and distraction, were calculated to foster his industry, and encourage him to efforts which were sure to be appreciated. To have an orchestra, his own orchestra too, which he was allowed to strengthen and improve until it was capable of rendering to perfection his highest efforts, at his absolute disposal every day and at any hour, was a boon for which many a musician would barter a good deal of his independence, and Haydn himself fully appreciated the advantages of his situation when he said, "My prince was always satisfied with my works. I not only had the encouragement of constant approval, but as conductor of an orchestra I could make experiments, observe what produced an effect and what weakened it, and was thus in a position to improve, alter, make additions and omissions, and be as bold as I pleased. I was cut off from the world, there was no one to confuse or torment me, and I was forced to become original." The following is a translation of the agreement in question, which gives us more than one curious picture of the manners and customs of the great men of the day and their dependants :—

FORM OF AGREEMENT AND INSTRUCTIONS FOR THE VICE-CAPELLMEISTER.

"This day (according to the date hereto appended) Joseph Heyden, native of Rohrau in Austria, is accepted and appointed Vice-Capellmeister in the service of his Serene Highness Paul Anton, Prince of the Holy Roman Empire, of Esterhazy and Galantha, &c. &c., with the conditions here following :—

"1. Seeing that the Capellmeister at Eisenstadt, by name Gregorius Werner, having devoted many years of true and faithful service to the princely house, is now on account of his great age and infirmities unfit to perform the duties incumbent on him, therefore the said Gregorius Werner, in consideration of his long services, shall retain the post of Capellmeister, and the said Joseph Heyden as Vice-Capellmeister shall, as far as regards the music of the choir, be subordinate to the Capellmeister and receive his instructions. But in everything else relating to musical performances, and in all that concerns the orchestra, the Vice-Capellmeister shall have the sole direction.

"2. The said Joseph Heyden shall be considered and treated as a member of the household. Therefore his Serene Highness is graciously pleased to place confidence in his conducting himself as becomes an honourable official of a princely house. He must be temperate, not showing himself overbearing towards his musicians, but mild and lenient, straightforward and composed. It is especially to be observed that when the orchestra shall be summoned to perform before company, the Vice-Capellmeister and all the musicians shall appear in uniform, and the said Joseph Heyden shall take care that he and all members of his orchestra do follow the instructions given, and appear in white stockings, white linen, powdered, and either with a pigtail or a tie-wig.

"3. Seeing that the other musicians are referred for directions to the said Vice-Capellmeister, therefore he should take the more care to conduct himself in an exemplary manner, abstaining from undue familiarity, and from vulgarity in eating, drinking, and conversation, not dispensing with the respect due to him, but acting uprightly and influencing his subordinates to preserve such harmony as is becoming in them, remembering how displeasing the consequences of any discord or dispute would be to his Serene Highness.

"4. The said Vice-Capellmeister shall be under an obligation to compose such music as his Serene Highness may command, and neither to communicate such compositions to any other person, nor to allow them to be copied, but to retain them for the absolute use of his Highness, and not to compose anything for any other person without the knowledge and permission of his Highness.

"5. The said Joseph Heyden shall appear in the antechamber daily, before and after midday, and inquire whether his Highness is pleased to order a performance of the orchestra. After receipt of his orders he shall communicate them to the other musicians, and shall take care to be punctual at the appointed time, and to ensure punctuality in his subordinates, making a note of those who arrive late or absent themselves altogether.

"6. Should any quarrel or cause of complaint arise, the Vice-Capellmeister shall endeavour to arrange it, in order that his Serene Highness may not be incommoded with trifling disputes; but should any more serious difficulty occur, which the said Joseph Heyden is unable to set right, his Serene Highness must then be respectfully called upon to decide the matter.

"7. The said Vice-Capellmeister shall take careful charge of all music and musical instruments, and shall be responsible for any injury that may occur to them from carelessness or neglect.

"8. The said Joseph Heyden shall be obliged to instruct the female vocalists, in order that they may not forget in the country what they have been taught with much trouble and expense in Vienna, and, as the said Vice-Capellmeister is proficient on various instruments, he shall take care to practise himself on all that he is acquainted with.

"9. A copy of this agreement and instructions shall be given to the said Vice-Capellmeister and to his subordinates, in order that he may be able to hold them to their obligations therein laid down.

"10. It is considered unnecessary to detail the services required of the said Joseph Heyden, more particularly since his Serene Highness is pleased to hope that he will of his own free will strictly observe not only these regulations, but all others that may from time to time be made by his Highness, and that he will place the orchestra on such a footing, and in such good order, that he may bring honour upon himself and deserve the further favour of the prince his master, who thus confides in his zeal and discretion.

"11. A salary of 400 florins to be received quarterly is hereby bestowed upon the said Vice-Capellmeister by his Serene Highness.

"12. In addition the said Joseph Heyden shall have board at the officers' table, or half a gulden a day in lieu thereof.

"13. Finally, this agreement shall hold good for at least three years from May 1st, 1761, with the further condition that if at the conclusion of this term the said Joseph Heyden shall desire to leave the service, he shall notify his intention to his Highness half a year beforehand.

"14. His Serene Highness undertakes to keep Joseph Heyden in his service during this time, and should he be satisfied with him, he may look forward to being appointed Capellmeister. This, however, must not be understood to deprive his Serene Highness of the freedom to dismiss the said Joseph Heyden at the expiration of the term, should he see fit to do so.

"Duplicate copies of this document shall be executed and exchanged.
"Given at Vienna this first day of May, 1761.
"Ad mandatum Celsissimi Principis,
"JOHANN STIFFTELL, *Secretary*."

It was a well-meant but somewhat mistaken kindness that suffered so old a servant of the house as Werner to retain his post as nominal head of the orchestra, while virtually superseding him by one whom he must have considered as a mere boy, and whose innovations and reforms must have been a constant source of vexation to him. Gregorius Josephus Werner had been appointed Capellmeister in 1728 by the Princess Maria Octavia Esterhazy, regent during the long minority of her son Paul Anton. Of his private life nothing is known beyond the fact that he was married to a wife accomplished enough to give lessons in music, and that he had several children, who all died young. His wife dying in 1753, the rest of his life was devoted to his official duties, and, after Haydn's appearance on the scene, to compositions chiefly religious, and all in the strictest form of the old school of counterpoint. Both he and Haydn seem to have accepted their relative positions with considerable good sense and forbearance. Although the elder and less liberal man not unfrequently characterized his Vice-Capellmeister as "a mere fop," and "a scribbler of songs," he had the wisdom to retire gradually and with a tolerably good grace from the active direction of the music, seeking consolation in the works (now almost forgotten) which were to carry his name down to posterity. Haydn always expressed, and we can see no reason for doubting that he felt, a sincere respect and admiration for his predecessor. Long years after Werner's death, when Haydn himself was an old man with a fame beyond the reach of rivalry, he published "Six Fugues by G. J. Werner, formerly Capellmeister to H.S.H. Prince N. Esterhazy, &c., arranged as string quartets by his successor, Joseph Haydn, out of sincere esteem for this celebrated master. Vienna : Artaria & Co.,

1804." Werner's industry as a composer is proved by the number of his works preserved among the Esterhazy archives, of which the following is a summary:—39 Masses, 3 Requiems, 12 Oratorios for Good Friday, 3 Te Deums, 4 Offertories, 12 Vespers, Psalms, Veni Sancte, 16 Hymns, 20 Litanies, 133 Antiphones, 14 Regina Cœli, 14 Alma Redemptoris, 5 Ave Regina, 9 Salve Regina, besides Responses, Rorate Cœli, Sub tuum, Miserere, Lamentations, Advent and Christmas songs in one, two, or more parts, pastorals, church sonatas, organ sonatas, &c.

Such fame, however, as Werner possesses at the present day is founded not upon these serious compositions, which are obsolete in style, and far too difficult ever to be well known, but on his popular and somewhat boisterous musical burlesques of Vienna life. Such are : 1. The Old Clothes Market of Vienna (4 voices, 2 violins, and bass); 2. The Election of a Village Justice (5 voices, 2 violins, and bass); 3. "A new and very curious musical Instrumental Calendar, for 2 violins and bass, divided into twelve parts denoting the twelve months, each described according to its kind and qualities, with oddities and original inventions by Gregorius Josephus Werner." All these were published at Augsburg in 1748. Werner lived under the new regime for five years, dying on March 3rd, 1766. His epitaph, written by himself, prays that the discords which have crept into his life may, by his contrition and penance, be resolved into harmonies, and that the last chord which finds its echo in his grave may die away into peace, until the trump of doom shall summon the world to judgment, when he trusts that he may find mercy, and ends by begging the passer-by to stop and pray for his soul.

At the time when Haydn entered upon his office, Prince Paul Anton was a man of fifty years of age. His career had been brilliant, and partly by inheritance, partly in reward of his services during the Seven Years' War, he had acquired immense possessions, and had been elevated to the dignity of Field-Marshal. Twice he had equipped and maintained during a whole campaign a complete regiment of hussars for the service of his royal mistress, and to his military fame was added a reputation for a genuine and enlightened love of the fine arts. Inheriting a talent for music from his mother, he acquired considerable skill on the violin, and spared no trouble to improve the condition of his Capelle, setting himself not so much to strengthen the numbers of his musicians, as to encourage them to perfect performances. Haydn found only sixteen members at his orders, including vocalists and instrumentalists. The orchestra was strengthened on particular occasions by pressing into the service any member of the household who could play on an instrument. We find also the schoolmasters of the neighbouring villages summoned to perform on the bassoon, and the tutor attached to the palace and his wife were expressly engaged to sing in the choir. The prosperous days of the Esterhazy Capelle began in 1760, when Prince Paul Anton took up his permanent residence at Eisenstadt. At no other point in its history could it so well have served the purpose of a young and aspiring genius, longing for materials on which to exercise his inventive skill and develop the ideas that burned within him for expression.

Prince Paul Anton was not destined to reap the reward of his discriminating choice of a Vice-Capellmeister. He died on March 18th, 1762, before Haydn had been in office for a year, and was succeeded by his brother Nicolaus, the Prince Esterhazy best known to the world outside his own country, who by his lavish display of wealth, and generous patronage of the fine arts, earned for himself, like Lorenzo de Medici, the title of " The Magnificent." The sensation that was created by his well-known diamond-covered coat will occur to most of our readers, although it would be doing him an injustice to take for granted that either his own ambition or the esteem of his contemporaries was bounded by such an exhibition of mere barbaric pomp. He was, there can be no doubt, a man of liberal mind and genial temper. His friends loved him, his dependants adored him. Haydn stood towards him in both these capacities, and in all the years during which they lived under the same roof, we can find no proof of anything happening to mar the respect, admiration, and sympathy of the master on the one hand, and the genuine devotion and hearty zeal of the servant on the other. Every now and then Haydn would lament his inability to travel in Italy, and so enlarge his range of musical ideas. He felt his confinement in Esterhaz as something like imprisonment, and longed for companionship with his fellow-artists in Vienna. But on such occasions he quickly consoled himself by remembering his resolution " to live and die " in the service of his prince, and, as we have seen, he was quite alive to the counterbalancing advantages of his position. Prince Nicolaus was of stately and commanding appearance, with an open and amiable expression of face. Although eminently fitted to shine at court, he withdrew more and more from the circle of its attractions, and after the completion of his palace at Esterhaz he hardly ever left it for Vienna. When he was forced to appear there, his anxiety to return caused him to break off his visits in the most abrupt manner, to the despair of his Capelle, and especially of Haydn, to whom these opportunities of intercourse with other composers and interchange of musical ideas became increasingly precious.

Before proceeding to an account of Haydn's long years of life and work at Eisenstadt and Esterhaz, it will be well to give our readers some idea of his personal appearance, and the impression he made upon those with whom he was most closely associated. He was within a few days of his thirtieth birthday when Prince Nicolaus succeeded his brother. We may imagine him as he appeared in his uniform of light blue and silver, knee-breeches, white stockings, lace ruffles, and white neckcloth. He always wore a wig with side curls and a pigtail, and retained the same fashion to the day of his death. Dies, Griesinger, and others of his biographers give a description of his personal appearance which confirms the best portraits extant. Dies says, " Haydn was below the middle height, and his legs were somewhat too short for his body, a defect rendered more noticeable by the style of his dress, which he steadily refused to change with the changes of fashion. His features were regular, his expression animated, yet at the same time temperate, gentle, and attractive. His face wore a stern look when in repose, but in conversation it was smiling and cheerful. I never heard him laugh out loud. His build was substantial, but deficient in muscle." His nose was aquiline, and disfigured by a polypus, which he always refused to have removed, and his face was deeply pitted with the smallpox. This also was probably the cause of his dark complexion, which earned him the *sobriquet* of "the Moor." His under-lip was large and hanging, his jaw massive, and this suggested to Lavater the lines which he wrote, according to his custom, under the *silhouette* of Haydn in his collection of celebrities.

Something out of the common I see in the eyes and the nose:
The brow too is lofty and good, but the mouth and the chin are
    Philistine.

Haydn considered himself an ugly man, and congratulated himself on the fact that it must be for something deeper than beauty that so many women fell in love with him. In truth, he took considerable pains to attract the fairer sex, and was never at a loss for a compliment. He carried neatness and cleanliness to an extreme, both in his person and his house. To the day of his death he would never receive visitors without being fully dressed, and the arrangement of his room and his papers was so exact and methodical, that any removal caused him much annoyance. The plan of daily life which he laid down for himself in his eighteenth year he continued with very little alteration to the end of his life. It was one of incessant industry with very little relaxation, and might serve to prove the exception to the rule which characterizes all genius as fitful and irregular. Haydn spoke in the broad Austrian dialect, and his conversation was sprinkled with the naive and humorous turns of expression common to the Austrian people. He spoke Italian fluently, French a little. He picked up some knowledge of English during his two visits to England, and of Latin he knew enough to compose the church services. He was exceedingly fond of fun, which was sometimes not over refined in its nature, but that he had a true sense of humour is proved by such compositions as the Farewell Symphony, or the "Surprise" Andante, which are the musical expression of essentially humorous ideas. His talent Haydn looked upon as the gift of God, to be freely used in His service. His piety was simple and sincere; when he was composing the "Creation," he said that he knelt down every day and prayed to God to strengthen him for his work. The cheerfulness of his church compositions is no sign of a frivolous mind, but, as he said to Carpani, " at the thought of God his heart leapt for joy, and he could not help his music doing the same." Children were always fond of Haydn—Papa Haydn as they called him, and there would doubtless have been less to complain of in his conduct as a husband, if he had been also a father. Of his generous appreciation of the works of other composers, and his readiness to recognize merit wherever it was to be found, many instances will occur as his life proceeds; and it is pleasant to think that in this particular Haydn does not stand alone among musicians. We have seen already how generously Emanuel Bach recognized Haydn's genius, and we can imagine no pleasanter picture than that of Mozart at the Thomas Schule listening in rapt delight to the singing of Bach's motets, and exclaiming: "That is indeed something to take a lesson from!" or Beethoven on his deathbed roused into animation at the sight of a lithograph of Haydn's birthplace, murmuring to the bystanders, " Strange that so great a man should have had so poor a home!"

But it is time that we returned to Haydn and his orchestra at Eisenstadt. A new epoch began with the rule of Prince Nicolaus, and neither Haydn nor his musicians were suffered to find the time hang heavy on their hands. Their zeal was stimulated by the enthusiasm and generosity of the prince. All the salaries were raised; Haydn received 600 florins instead of 400, and this was soon after raised to 782 (about 78*l*.). The Kapelle now numbered twenty-one members male and female, seven vocalists, and fourteen instrumentalists. The principal were Luigi Tomasini (violin), Jos. Weigl (cello), Thadäus Steinmüller (French horn), Anna Maria Scheffstos (soprano), and Karl Friberth (tenor).

Haydn had everything to arrange. Stage, instruments, music-books, even the boxes to keep them in, all were under his personal care. Compositions, rehearsals, concerts, disputes to settle among the musicians and petitions to present to the prince filled up his busy days, and it would seem that even some portion of the copying of his compositions was done by his own hand to avoid applying for more money to the prince. The mild and courteous rule of Nicolaus was taken advantage of by some of his musicians, who became careless in their attendance, and sometimes unseemly in their conduct. Then followed punishments, fines, suspensions, and occasional dismissals, almost invariably followed by a petition for pardon and reinstatement for the culprit from Haydn, whose soft heart was touched by the least sign of contrition. There is still extant a petition on behalf of an offender from the prince's "most obedient and faithful Haydn," with a postscript following without a pause to allow the prince to take breath : "who will venture to submit to his Highness immediately after the holidays a new trio for the barytone." Happy the dependants of a prince who could be so easily and innocently bribed to show mercy !

For the first five years after his appointment Haydn's life passed thus peacefully and busily at Eisenstadt. Once indeed in 1765 he was taken to task by his princely master for want of industry in composition, and for failing to maintain proper discipline among his musicians; but as a very few weeks after we find the prince writing to his steward to reward Haydn with twelve ducats for three pieces he had just received, and with which he was "very much pleased," we must conclude that the reproof was taken in good part; certainly, as far as we know, it was never repeated.

On three occasions the monotony of life in the palace was broken by festivities which gave Haydn opportunity for showing his skill in operatic compositions. Forgotten as these now are, he himself was not inclined to rank them below his other works, although he acknowledged that apart from their original surroundings they would fail to produce their calculated effect.

As soon as the days of mourning for Prince Paul Anton and for his mother Maria Octavia, who died in the following month, were over, Prince Nicolaus made his triumphal entry into Eisenstadt. The festivities continued for a whole month, during which a company of "foreign players" were lodged in the village inn, and performed on a stage erected in the large conservatory. For this company Haydn wrote several operettas, of which one, "La Marchesa Nepola" still exists in autograph score. The words are poor and unconnected, and the music shows signs of haste and disinclination, even the handwriting being far less careful than is usually the case with Haydn. His second dramatic essay at Eisenstadt was on a larger scale. The occasion was the betrothal of Prince Nicolaus's eldest son, Anton, in January, 1763, with the Countess Maria Theresa, daughter of Count Nicolaus Erdödy. The ceremony was performed at Vienna by the Archbishop of Colossa, and the festivities which immediately followed at Eisenstadt were on a scale of regal magnificence. Banquets, illuminations, balls, and masquerades continued without intermission for several days, and the guests were at a loss whether to admire most the splendour of the entertainments or the high-bred ease and courtesy of their host. The people had a considerable share in the general rejoicings. On the day after the arrival of the company they were entertained in the park, in the open air, and on the same day after dinner Haydn's Italian operetta (Festa Teatrale) "Acide" was performed by members of the Kapelle, the orchestra being in all the glory of a new uniform of crimson and gold. The subject was the old myth of the loves of the sea-nymph Galatea and the shepherd Acis, and the jealous vengeance of Polyphemus. Handel had already made it the text of one of his most charming compositions, but with a chorus at his disposal he was able to render it a far more important work than that of Haydn, who had to resort to an awkward manœuvring of the text in order to close the last scene with a quartet. Of Haydn's music to "Acide" there still remain in autograph score the overture (except the first thirty-two bars), four arias, and the finale quartet. The overture is in his own style, fresh and cheerful, foreshadowing his symphonies. The songs are in the Italian manner, very inferior in originality and expression to Handel's music; the quartet is crude in form and uninteresting in substance.

In 1764, Prince Nicolaus left Eisenstadt to attend the coronation of the Archduke Joseph at Frankfort, and as soon as the festivities following the ceremony were at an end, he continued his journey to Paris, where he made a great sensation by his lavish display of wealth and magnificence. It was during this visit no doubt that, fired with the idea of emulating the splendour and beauty of Versailles, he planned the conversion of his own estate of Esterhaz into a rival of the French paradise.

The Prince's return to Eisenstadt was made an occasion of rejoicing, and Haydn seems to have been specially forward in displaying his zeal and devotion. He composed a Te Deum for the chapel and a cantata for the great hall. The actual performance of these works seems to have been postponed until the celebration of the prince's birthday, but the words of the cantata prove it to have been written as a welcome home. In a long recitative, two arias, duets, and choruses it glorifies the power and the virtues of the prince, prays for his happiness, and rejoices in his favour. Parts of the cantata were afterwards made use of in church services, but the work follows the traditional taste of the age in such compositions too closely for the display of any originality or real power.

Of Haydn's private life during the five years we are considering there is little to be said. His wife was only occasionally with him, one of the standing grievances of the Capelle being that the prince's exceptional love of his country residence separated them for long periods from their families and homes. Haydn would scarcely join in the complaint, although he afterwards proved his ability to sympathize with it. A pleasant event in 1762 was the appointment of his brother Michael as Concertmeister and director of the orchestra to Archbishop Sigismund at Salzburg. Here in 1768 he married Maria Magdalena Lipp, one of the court singers, and here, too, he was thrown into close intercourse with Leopold Mozart and his son Wolfgang, then ten years of age, and already exciting astonishment by his compositions. The personal relations between the two families were not over friendly. Michael Haydn was a man of no refinement or cultivation, and his wife's conduct was not free from reproach. But personal differences never affected Mozart's judgment as an artist, nor prevented his doing a kind action when occasion arose. He admired and carefully studied Michael Haydn's church music, much of which he copied with his own hand, and twenty years later we have a pleasant glimpse of him seated by Haydn's sick-bed, writing in the midst of a press of other work two duets, which the composer's illness prevented his writing, and which he was bound to have ready by a certain day, under penalty of dismissal by the Archbishop.

One other family event belongs to this period, which, to a heart so warm and with so tender a memory of early days as that of Haydn, must have been a source of keen sorrow. Mathias Haydn had had the satisfaction of seeing his dearest hopes realized. He had visited his son at Eisenstadt, had heard him addressed as Herr Capellmeister, and been a witness of the respect and esteem in which he was held by his prince and his orchestra. We can imagine the pride with which he would dilate to his friends at Rohrau upon Joseph's fame, and the splendour amidst which he lived. But no very long time after his return home, a log of wood falling on him as he was at work, struck his chest, and broke several ribs. Of the injuries thus inflicted he died on September 12th, 1763. Johann Evangelist, his youngest son by his first marriage, was still at home, but two years later, he being then twenty-two years of age, Joseph sent for him to Eisenstadt, and he was admitted into the choir. He had neither voice nor talent, however, and his career was not prosperous. His delicate health obliged him to make constant appeals for help to his brother, who was never deaf to such calls, and aided him both in money and by sending him pupils. Once, and once only, in 1801, the three brothers met at Eisenstadt. They dined together, and walked arm-in-arm through the streets. In the evening a serenade composed for the occasion was performed under their window by members of the orchestra.

CHAPTER IV.

WORKS AT EISENSTADT.

1760—1766.

For the first five years following his appointment as Vice-Capellmeister, Haydn's life at Eisenstadt continued without any break, except his occasional visits to Vienna in the train of his prince, or any noteworthy incident, except such inspirations to composition as were afforded by the prince's absence and return from a short stay abroad, or the marriage of his son, both of which events we have already noted. The death of Capellmeister Werner, and the completion of Prince Nicolaus's palace of Esterhaz mark the year 1766 as a fresh starting-point in Haydn's career, and it will be well, before following his fortunes in his new position and new home, briefly to pass in review the compositions, vocal and instrumental, which were the fruit of his five years of labour at Eisenstadt. Of his Italian operettas (1762), his "Acide e Galatea" (1763), and his cantata in honour of Prince Nicolaus's return to Eisenstadt (1764), mention has already been made. The only other vocal works of importance which can with certainty be ascribed to this period are the Te Deum in C major, composed for the same occasion as the cantata just alluded to, and a Salve Regina in G major, of which a copy dated 1766 is still in existence. The Te Deum is a complete and carefully worked-out composition for four voices and the somewhat scanty orchestra at his command; the instrumentation is fresh and vigorous without undue elaboration, and it is interesting to compare this early work with Haydn's great Te Deum in C major, composed for four voices and a full orchestra in 1800, when he was at the zenith of his fame. The comparison will confirm its authorship as that of Joseph Haydn, which has sometimes been disputed in favour of his brother Michael. The Salve Regina, for soprano and alto solo voices, with violin and organ accompaniment, is in three short movements, the middle movement being for alto alone; it is full of grace and melody, and breathes the gentle piety which befits a petition to the Virgin.

The instrumental compositions falling within these five years are very numerous, comprising about thirty symphonies and cassations, six divertimenti, eighteen quartets, six string trios, a piece for four violins and cello called "Echo," a concerto for the French horn, twelve minuets for the orchestra, and concertos, trios, sonatas, and variations for the clavier.

The circumstances under which Haydn's early symphonies were composed must be taken into account before commenting on the astonishing number which he produced, and the want of that depth of feeling and solemnity of treatment which Mozart and Beethoven to a still greater degree have taught us to look for in what became under their hands the very highest expression of musical emotion, pure and simple. Haydn's symphonies were composed in groups of four, six, or seven, for those musical performances which were the customary evening entertainments of the wealthy nobility, and only so much variety was required as should avoid actual repetition or monotony in the successive groups of movements. The performances were long, and included a great deal of orchestral music. Count Firmian's musical *soirées* lasted from five to eleven o'clock, and on one evening several symphonies by J. C. Bach and four symphonies by Martini were played. Dittersdorf tells us in his autobiography that he once played twelve new violin concertos by Benda on one evening, and at a private concert in Dresden both parts contained a symphony, a violin concerto, a flute concerto, and an oboe concerto. Haydn's peculiar services to music can hardly be said to have suffered from the obligation to fertility which was the consequence of his position. It was his mission to stereotype the forms and develop the capacities of instrumental music, more especially of its two chief exponents, the symphony and the quartet. Within his own limits, his invention was inexhaustible, his originality knew no bounds, but his aim was no higher than that of other great composers before Beethoven, who sought to display the beauties of music only within its own domain of sound. Mozart's achievements are the highest and greatest possible within those limits; it was reserved for Beethoven to break down the barrier between music and poetry, and in his symphonies to celebrate, as it were, the apotheosis of instrumental music, showing the aim of the musician henceforth to be the expression in sound of the joys, aspirations, and longings of the poet. With Beethoven the older school of instrumental music, the school of Bach, Handel, Haydn, Mozart, came to an end; no further progress in it was possible; his genius, "Titanically infantine," has been "laid at the breast of the Divine," and for better, for worse, music has now recognized its mission as an accompaniment to the drama of humanity with its griefs, its joys, and its passions. Recognizing this fact, however, to its fullest extent, it will still remain the case that, as long as men have ears that are refreshed by melody, as long as they can still understand the definition of music as "a concord of sweet sounds," they will not cease to find pleasure in Haydn's symphonies and quartets. "How Haydn-ish!" we say, as the flood of melody comes pouring out, clear and fresh and bright as a mountain stream; our brows relax, and our hearts lighten as we listen; nor can our intellects fail to be satisfied with the perfect design, the finished workmanship, the subservience of all means to one end which are unfolded as the work proceeds. When it ends we feel that we have been in the presence of a master of his art, and in proportion as our musical knowledge and feeling are real and deep we can understand the reverence with which Haydn's claims to be the father of instrumental music have been acknowledged by his contemporaries and successors.

The term "symphony" was applied to more than one form of instrumental composition in vogue during the last century. The word was used as synonymous with overture, and it was some time before the connection between the symphony and the opera to which it served as an introduction was severed. The French symphony, introduced by Lulli (1633—1687), and established by Scarlatti and his followers, began with an adagio, followed by a quick movement, often in the form of a fugue, and passed again into an adagio, which concluded the overture. The Italian symphony had three movements: an allegro at the beginning, and another quicker and more animated at the end, separated by a slow movement. Burney says that the composers of the celebrated Mannheim Capelle, who were all of the first rank, first overstepped the usual limits of the opera overture, which hitherto had only consisted of a sort of summons to silence and attention on the entry of the singers, and completed the development of the symphony as an independent composition. But Sammartini and Pallavicini in Italy had already done good service to orchestral music and to the symphony as its principal exponent, and Haydn surpassed them all in his inexhaustible wealth of productive power and thorough knowledge of his art, and may justly be considered the creator of the symphony.

In the complete form thus given to the symphony, the original three movements of the Italian overture were preserved, but they were no longer (or only occasionally) connected, and on the formation of the separate movements the clavier sonata in the perfect form given to it by Ph. Emanuel Bach had a very considerable influence. The few bars of adagio which precede the allegro in many of Haydn's symphonies is perhaps a reminiscence of the French symphony. The allegro itself is always in two parts; in the first part the principal and secondary subjects are set forth and contrasted, and sometimes they are followed by a third, the whole connected by means of free passages. The first subject closes on the sub-dominant, and the second is in the key of the dominant, in which the first part of the movement concludes.

The second part consists of an elaboration of the subjects already given, carried out in various ways, and without any very definite rule. This " working out " part asserts itself more and more as the nucleus of the movement, and has an important reaction on the formation and phrasing of the first part; this comes to be regarded as the foundation prepared for the development which first displays the whole extent of the conception. After the working out, the first part is repeated with modifications of key, and provides a clear and satisfying conclusion to the movement, like the summing-up of a verbal argument. The coda which ends the whole is usually confined to a lengthened development of the closing phrase, and has its counterpart in vocal music in the cadenza of the aria.

The middle movement is slow in tempo, and simple in design and composition, following the lines of the operatic cavatina, the romanze, or the *Lied*. It has one main subject, either with variations or embellishments, and is generally, though not necessarily, divided into two parts, the second consisting of a new statement of the subject rather than a development of it. The slow movement long continued to be of minor importance in instrumental compositions, and the adagio in its most perfect form is a later and an essentially German creation. Modern musicians do not excel in this particular direction, and Schumann, who repeatedly remarks on the phenomenon, considers that it is an extinct branch of musical art, and that a new character must be invented for middle movements.

The closing movement of the symphony is always in a lively time and measure, generally in rondo form very freely treated, and was expected to produce a feeling of enjoyment and leave a pleasant impression on the mind. But, curiously enough, this movement was sometimes made the vehicle for a display of skill in counterpoint, the very difficulty of rendering cheerfulness and unrestrained musical fun in the strictest possible forms, making the attraction of the task.

The introduction of the minuet as a fourth movement of the symphony was probably suggested by the suite, and whether or not Haydn first introduced it, it was undoubtedly he who gave it an individual and typical character. The minuet was the dance of good society, the appropriate music suggesting the dignified deportment and courtly grace of the age of powder and hoops.

Haydn divested his minuets of this high-bred air of dignity, and filled them instead with the cheerful goodhumour of the *bourgeois* of his day, without a taint of vulgarity or carelessness of construction. He retained the form, but changed the spirit; and the minuet, as he made it, took its place in the symphony and kept it. In these movements more, perhaps, than in any other, we are delighted with his humorous turns of expression, his constant flow of cheerful melody, and a fertility of invention which is the more astonishing when we reflect that his compositions of this particular kind must be numbered by hundreds.

A careful study of Haydn's earlier symphonies shows that he had spent his long years of struggle with poverty in mastering the technicalities of his art, and that he had already made up his mind on all essential points connected with the forms of instrumental music. But it will scarcely be expected that these works, composed for all sorts of occasions, and often at very short notice, shall all be found of equal merit and importance. Some of them are not, properly speaking, symphonies at all, but should rather be classed as divertimenti or cassations (a term which has never been satisfactorily explained), compositions not so fixed in form as symphonies, containing a greater number of movements, and in which the various parts are more simply arranged. Anything like a detailed account of Haydn's symphonies, or even a mere enumeration of them under their separate titles would be impossible within reasonable limits, but before passing on to his other compositions of this period, it will be found of interest to say a few words on the first symphony (C major), composed at Eisenstadt, usually entitled "Le Midi," to which Haydn afterwards added another, "Le Matin," and a concertino, " Le Soir." Haydn seems to have determined at once to take his prince, his orchestra, and his Capellmeister by storm. The unusual number of parts in the score must have necessitated the strengthening of the orchestra, as it was then constituted, by the engagement of special musicians from Vienna; and the constant and unusual employment of obbligato instruments, especially the long dramatic recitative for the violin inserted between the first allegro and the adagio, must have caused poor old Werner to throw up his hands in holy horror at such startling innovations. The symphony is in the usual four movements, preceded by a few bars of solemn adagio by way of introduction. The first allegro is unusually rich in subjects and carefully worked out. The violin recitative is very remarkable, the more so from its want of connection with either of the neighbouring movements. It is difficult to avoid imagining that Haydn intended to embody in it some definite idea. Dr. Pohl, with an apology for adopting the vicious practice of attempting to give verbal expression to the musical meaning of a composer, suggests the idea of an accused person before his judge. It is, at any rate, full of dignity, and has a breadth of dramatic expression not hitherto displayed by Haydn. It was actually suggested, doubtless, by the recent engagement as first violin of Luigi Tomasini, who, although then only in his twentieth year, had already given promise of becoming a first-rate artist. He remained a member of the Esterhazy Capelle until his death in 1808, and his services to Haydn, and through him to the world, can hardly be overrated, inasmuch as his talent and zeal afforded the master an incentive to compositions which were sure of being ably rendered by the disciple. "No one plays my quartets as you do," said Haydn to him, and their relations throughout were those of mutual admiration and affection.

This first symphony in C major has, curiously enough, never been included in Breitkopf's catalogue, and only appeared in Hamburg in 1782, and in Vienna in 1799. Haydn's autograph score (dated 1761) is, however, preserved in Eisenstadt, and bears, like other of his early compositions, the superscription, *In Nomine Domini*, and after the final signature, *Laus Deo*, Haydn's customary close.

We are reminded of the J. J. (Jesu Juva), with which J. S. Bach dedicated all his works to the service of God. Haydn retained the custom, even for his secular works and opera scores. Sometimes he merely added the initials *L.D.* or *S.D.G.* (Soli Deo Gloria). Occasionally we find *B.V.M.* (Beatæ Virgini Mariæ); and the most emphatic close of all is that to his opera, " L'Infedeltà delusa : " *Laus omnipotenti Deo et Beatissimæ Virgini Mariæ.*

The smaller orchestral compositions of this period of Haydn's life, variously called Divertimenti, Cassations, Serenate or Notturni, Concertine, Scherzandi, and Partite, are not very easily distinguishable in form and composition. They all consist of three, four, or sometimes more movements grouped together without any fixed rule, and the different names given to them seem to have applied more to the occasions for which they were written than to the works themselves. Written to order, and without any pretence to high aim or great conception, they are interesting to musicians mainly as forming an intermediate step between the symphony and the quartet. One divertimento, " à Echo," may be mentioned as an example of the kind of musical fun in which Haydn excelled. It is composed for a double trio of instruments (two violins and one violoncello), to be played in two rooms adjoining, the musicians to be so placed that they can see each other. The five movements (adagio, allegro, minuet, adazio, and presto) never go beyond the limits of a musical joke, composed for the amusement of a set of amateurs ; but the number of times and the different arrangements in which the piece was published, prove it to have been an especial favourite not only in Vienna, but in Paris, Italy, and Berlin. A word must also be said here on a style of composition much in favour towards the end of the 18th century, called " Harmoniemusik," for wind instruments alone. Sometimes it was in the form of serenades, and people of rank had performances of six or eight-part Harmoniemusik during meals. The Emperor Joseph, the Archduke Maximilian, and other princes had special orchestras for these concerts; and in after-years, during his visit to London, Haydn was greatly pleased with the wind band of the Prince of Wales under the conductorship of Christian Cramer. Most of Haydn's Harmoniemusik, or Tafelmusik, as it was sometimes called, belonging to these early years has been lost; it is from a much later composition of the kind that Johannes Brahms has taken the subject for his orchestral variations. Of the dance music composed by Haydn we have already spoken. His minuets for dancing were gayer and lighter than those for his symphonies, and although he has not included them in the autograph catalogue of his works, he evidently set some store by them. In 1790, he writes to his publisher, Artaria, offering him twelve " very capital minuets and trios" in payment of a debt of twelve ducats.

The quartet has long been acknowledged as the noblest and most perfect form of instrumental chamber music, and it was Haydn who gave to the quartet its characteristic form and developed it to such a degree of perfection that, as Goethe says, " he may be superseded, he can never be surpassed." The quartet became for Haydn the spontaneous expression of his musical nature, the fullest result of his life-work, and it is seldom indeed that an artist has been so successful in discovering the fittest outcome for his individual genius. Others before him had written compositions for four instruments; his contemporaries, J. C. Bach, Jomelli, Stamitz, Boccherini, and others, published quartets in the same collections in which his appeared; but it was his inexhaustibly fertile invention, his freedom in the treatment of form, his unerring judgment concerning the relative powers and capacities of each instrument which caused the quartet to become one of the most beautiful productions of German musical art. It was only by degrees that Haydn's contemporaries learned to appreciate the services rendered by his genius to this branch of his art. But he gradually gained the favour of the public, and secured the homage of his fellow-artists by an unbroken series of works advancing in depth of conception and finish of execution, until at last whoever ventured on the same field was obliged to serve under his banner. Here, again, Haydn acknowledged his obligations to Ph. Emánuel Bach, rather than to those of his predecessors who had actually composed for four instruments. The clavier sonata was again made his model, and the rules for the quartet became as definitely fixed as those for the symphony.

The quartet, as Haydn found it, differed little from the orchestral compositions of which we have just spoken. In fact, Haydn himself called his first quartets Cassations, Divertimenti, and Notturni. How he must have rejoiced to find them growing under his hand into what he could not but feel to be the truest and best expression of the genius that, as he said, was "in him"! The uniformity of the material element of sound in the string quartet, combined with an almost infinite capacity for variety of tone-colouring and individual movement among the instruments, render this the most agreeable development of chamber music.

"The favourite comparison of the quartet with a conversation between four intellectual persons holds good in some degree," says Otto Jahn,[1] "if it is kept in mind that the intellectual participation and sympathy of the interlocutors, although not necessarily languishing in conversation, are only audibly expressed by turns, whereas the musical embodiment of ideas must be continuous and simultaneous. The comparison is intended to illustrate the essential point that every component part of the quartet stands out independently according to its character, but so diffidently that all cooperate to produce a whole which is never at any moment out of view; an effect so massive as to absorb altogether the individual parts would be as much out of place as the undue emphasizing of any one part, and the subordination of the others to it."

The eighteen quartets composed by Haydn during the years of which we are speaking, and those immediately following, display in a striking manner his gradual development in inventive power, definite aim, and breadth of

[1] "Life of Mozart" (Eng. Edit.), vol. iii. p. 9.

treatment. It has been questioned whether he wished them to be included among his later works of the same kind, which are in strict quartet form, and Artaria's thematic catalogue of the quartets begins, according to Haydn's desire, Artaria said, with the nineteenth (Op. 9, No. 1). But the total omission of these earlier works in any study of Haydn's quartets would be a very great mistake. They are absolutely necessary to a right understanding of his method and progress in this species of composition, nor will they ever cease to be sought after by all true lovers of music, not on account of their historic interest only, but for the wealth of melody, the purity of thought, and the innocent desire to give pleasure, which breathe from every movement.

Haydn's string trios were almost all composed early, and are wanting in individuality and breadth of design, throwing into striking relief the great advance in originality and power of expression made by him as soon as he had adopted the quartet for his own. The greater number of the twenty-one trios for two violins and one violoncello, which he includes in his catalogue, were composed before 1767. They are generally in three movements, adagio or allegro, minuet and presto, and the first violin is often made so prominent that they might rather be considered as violin solos with accompaniments for the other two instruments.

Haydn spent much of his time at Eisenstadt and Esterhaz in composing for the barytone, a stringed instrument closely resembling the viola di gamba, upon his skill on which Prince Nicolaus piqued himself considerably. It was Haydn's duty to compose as many pieces for the barytone as the prince required, and that it was somewhat of a forced task may be inferred from the reproof for idleness administered by the prince, of which mention has already been made, wherein Vice-Capellmeister Haydn was commanded to show himself more industrious than heretofore in the composition chiefly of "such pieces as could be played on the gamba." The reproof was almost immediately followed by a reward of twelve ducats for three pieces, with which the prince was "very well pleased." Haydn's zealous attempt to surprise and delight his master by learning to perform on the instrument himself was by no means so successful. His intended surprise was received with a cold indifference which amounted to disapprobation; he took the hint and never again sought to rival the prince. Of the 163 barytone compositions included in his own thematic catalogue, the greater number were written after 1766; but it may be as well to consider them all together here, as they show no marked difference in style and treatment. Many of them are trios for barytone, viola, and violoncello, generally in three movements, among which a minuet and trio are invariably included. Others are duets for two barytones,[2] or barytone and cello, or cassations for three or more instruments, but the larger number are divertimenti for baryton, viola, and violoncello.

Haydn did not suffer himself to compose carelessly even such trifling pieces as these. He made them serve as studies for larger works, and many of them surpass in interest and variety his earlier quartets, being capable, even now, of affording real pleasure to amateurs of instrumental chamber music.

It now only remains to consider the music for the clavier which Haydn composed before 1766. His most youthful compositions were probably for this instrument written for his pupils in the days of his early struggle with poverty. Here, again, his knowledge and style were grounded on the works of Emanuel Bach, whose influence is as marked in this direction as in any other At the same time, a comparison between his clavier concertos and his quartets and symphonies shows very plainly that the clavier was not the instrument best fitted

---

[2] The second barytone was often played by Kraft, the violoncellist, who was no more fortunate than Haydn in an attempt to rival his master. Having introduced a solo for the second barytone in a composition which he presented to the prince, the latter asked to look at the part and began to try it over. Coming to a passage which he could not master, he exclaimed angrily, "For the future, write solos only for my part; it is no credit to you to play better than I; it is your duty."

for Haydn's genius. His individuality disappears as soon as he sets himself to write mere show pieces, and we can scarcely recognize as his the long movements spun out to tediousness with old-fashioned runs and ornamental passages which were put together with evident want of interest or care to form his earlier concertos. They are all in three movements, the slow one in the middle, the form which was adopted by J. S. Bach for his concertos, and which has remained the basis of such compositions to the present day. The solo instrument is accompanied by two violins, viola, and bass, with occasional horns or trumpets, and drums *ad lib.* One concerto (composed in 1766) has a solo violin, which plays alternate passages with the clavier, the accompaniment being somewhat fuller than usual. Another is catalogued by Haydn as " per l' organo;" but it has nothing sacred or ecclesiastical about it, and could at most have served as a voluntary for dismissal. It affords no standard for judging of Haydn's merits as an organ-player.

CHAPTER V.

ESTERHAZ.

1766—1790.

DURING the year 1766 two events of considerable importance broke the monotony of Haydn's life, which afterwards flowed on in the same even current as before. The first was the death of Capellmeister Werner, to which allusion has already been made. Haydn now became in name what he had long been in fact, absolute head of the Esterhazy Capelle, and the relief must have been great from the small daily annoyances of his former position, and the want of artistic sympathy between him and his nominal superior.

His promotion may be said to have placed Haydn at the goal of his early ambition, and a glow of pardonable pride may well have thrilled his heart as he read the following paragraph in the "Wiener Diarium" for 1766, and remembered that his own hard study and self-denial and his own inexhaustible fund of cheerful hopefulness and genial love of his art had placed him where he was, and given him already a fame and popularity spreading far beyond his own narrow sphere of duty. The paragraph in question, giving an account of the most noted musicians of Vienna, includes Haydn among the number, and describes him as "Herr Joseph Hayden, the favourite of our nation (der Liebling unserer Nation), whose amiable disposition speaks through every one of his works. His music has beauty, style, purity, and a delicate and noble simplicity which commends it to every hearer. His cassations, quartets, and trios may be compared to a pure, clear stream of water, the surface now rippled by a gentle breeze from the south, and anon breaking into agitated billows, but without ever leaving its proper channel and appointed course. His symphonies are full of force and delicate sympathy. In his cantatas he shows himself at once captivating and caressing, and in his minuets he is delightful and full of humour. In short, Haydn is in music what Gellert is in poetry." This comparison was at that time the most flattering that could be made, and may have suggested Dittersdorf's answer to Joseph II. in 1786, when the emperor requested him to draw an analogy between Haydn's and Mozart's chamber music. Dittersdorf answered by requesting the emperor in his turn to draw a parallel between Gellert and Klopstock; whereupon Joseph replied that both were great poets, but that Klopstock's works needed attentive study, while Gellert's beauties were open to the first glance. The analogy, Dittersdorf tells us, pleased the emperor very much.

Of still greater influence upon Haydn's well-being and musical progress, was the second event of the year 1766, the completion of Prince Nicolaus's famous Palace of Esterhaz, and the removal thither of his establishment, including the Capelle except the few voices necessary to conduct the church services at Eisenstadt. Ever since the prince's visit to Versailles, then, with its park and gardens and interior decorations, one of the wonders of the world, it had been his dream to construct for himself a palace, on entering which his visitors should spontaneously exclaim, "This is a second Versailles!" Nay, more than this, he chose for his purpose that one of all his numerous estates which offered least facility for transformation into a paradise. Esterhaz, or Süttor, as it had hitherto been called, lies on the south-east side of the Neusiedler See, that enormous salt-water lake, which on this side terminates in a morass called the Hansag, as great in extent as the lake itself. On this unhealthy marsh, the haunt of the wild fowl, and the scene of perpetual floods, Count Joseph Anton had built in 1720 a small and unpretentious hunting-lodge, and his passion for wild-fowl shooting, shared by his brother and successor, Prince Michael, made Süttor a favourite resort with them both. No improvement was made in the condition of the estate under the son of Prince Michael, Paul Anton, also an enthusiastic sportsman. Provided their passion for sport was allowed free indulgence, it mattered little to these princely autocrats that the few of their subjects who were forced to inhabit this deadly region crept about emaciated shadows, racked with ague and malaria, and only able to get a scanty subsistence from the ground. The improvement of the land would have been the destruction of their amusement, therefore the land remained a pestilential swamp until a prince reigned whose ambition it was to raise a second Versailles in the desert. The works, executed by order of Prince Nicolaus, were almost fabulous in their extent and magnificence, but many years passed before they were actually completed. It was not until 1781—1782, long after the palace was built and inhabited, that the district was drained by the construction of a dam across the marsh from the village of Pomaggen to the palace, upwards of five miles long, planted with trees on either side, and by the cutting of three canals, the chief of which is between seventeen and eighteen miles in length, and capable of bearing ships of considerable size. The plague-stricken swamp was by this means transformed into valuable pasture-land, and the palace was no longer the unsafe place of residence it had hitherto been. But it was impossible to render it really healthy, and it has long since been abandoned by the Esterhazys in favour of Eisenstadt. The unpretentious hunting-lodge of Count Joseph Anton was transformed by Prince Nicolaus into a palace containing 162 rooms, including a reception-hall in white marble, magnificently decorated in the style of Louis XV., and a still more beautiful summer hall, in which the musical performances were held on specially festive occasions. Almost every room in the palace contained costly and well-chosen examples of Japanese or Indian art, and the picture-gallery, filled with masterpieces of Italian and Dutch artists, was almost equalled in richness and interest by the library, with its invaluable collection of manuscripts, engravings, and rare prints.

The palace was surrounded by pleasure-gardens, laid out in the taste of the day, while the dense wood beyond was transformed into a perfect labyrinth of groves and glades adorned with summer-houses, temples, cascades, and statues, and intersected by paths in every direction. Two noble avenues of chestnut-trees extended to right and left of the palace. Facing the right avenue stood the opera-house and coffee-house adjoining, the usual rendezvous of the artistic world of Esterhaz. Opposite this was the Marionette Theatre, built like a grotto inside and out, the walls covered with sparkling stones and shells of every hue, giving a weird impression not unsuitable to the quaint drolleries of the performances there held. The opera—or play-house—was a building of considerable taste and importance, capable of seating about 500 guests. The stage was deep and wide, the scenery and costumes excellently appointed. Daily representations (entry being free to all the prince's retainers and servants, and to any strangers who might happen to be in the neighbourhood) were held in the theatre while the prince was in residence, and twice a week operatic performances were given.

The affection of Prince Nicolaus for Esterhaz increased as the years went on. He was never tired of altering, extending, and improving the palace and grounds, and his greatest ambition was to make the musical and theatrical entertainments there given the best of their kind in Europe. Eisenstadt he visited seldom; Vienna only when summoned thither on occasions of state, his only desire then being to return as quickly as possible to his beloved Esterhaz.

Haydn's life at Esterhaz was, as will be seen, one of almost complete retirement combined with incessant industry. The necessity of providing for two operatic performances and one or two concerts in every week, besides the daily music; the immense amount of preparation necessary for the festivities given in honour of distinguished visitors, of which music was the most prominent feature, besides the personal supervision of the Capelle and everything connected with it, which we know to have been expected from the Capellmeister; all this must have required no ordinary amount of industry and method to accomplish as Haydn accomplished it. His would seem to be an almost solitary instance of the perfection of these qualities combined with great original genius.

We are not surprised to find Prince Nicolaus raising the salary of so valuable a servant, granting his every request, and seeking by all the means in his power to make him contented with his position. When the prince went to Vienna, Haydn always accompanied him, and on rare occasions he was allowed short leave of absence to visit the capital alone. More and more precious, in proportion to their rarity, grew these peeps at the outer world of art and artists to the prisoner of Esterhaz. The prince too often brought his visits to an abrupt termination long before Haydn had heard and seen his fill of Vienna and music, and towards the close of his life they ceased altogether. There were times when Haydn felt his imprisonment sorely. His longing to visit Italy, his belief that a wider fame would open to him could he only reside in the capital, his distaste to the neighbourhood and climate of Esterhaz, are all poured out in his letters to his faithful friend, Frau v. Genzinger, and a glance at this shadier side of his life must lead us to admire anew the genius and energy which could produce a never-failing succession of works sparkling with originality and gaiety, under circumstances which would have overwhelmed many lesser minds with ennui and disgust. With his orchestra he was omnipotent and heartily beloved; he called them all his children, and to them he was always "Father Haydn." "*Friend!* go back to the first allegro," he writes as a direction on the music book of one of them, and the word was no mere title, but a reality. Unwearied as a conductor, he rehearsed until every passage went exactly to his mind, but without ever raising his voice in anger or impatience. He followed with gesture and expression every turn in the music, chuckling beforehand at the approach of a humorous passage, and betraying deeper emotion when it was called for. Interpolated embellishments he never allowed either in singers or instrumentalists: "I could have written it so myself if I had wished," he used to say when any such liberty was taken.

Haydn was not a proficient on any instrument, and rarely played solo. He had studied the violin with his early friend Dittersdorf sufficiently to take part in a quartet, and during one of his visits to Vienna, Kelly tells us of a quartet party at Storace's, when Haydn took the first violin, Dittersdorf the second (more probably these parts were reversed), Mozart tenor, and Vanhall violoncello. The clavier remained to the end of his life the instrument on which he tried his compositions, but he is only once mentioned as having performed on it in public, and that was during his visit to London in 1792. We have already seen what ill-success attended his attempt to please his prince by a performance on the barytone, a performance never repeated. He was fond of walking on Sunday mornings from Esterhaz to the village church of Szeplak to play the organ there, and he had a certain allowance in kind from the prince as deputy organist at Eisenstadt.

In a life of such incessant and varied industry as that of Haydn at Esterhaz, his habit of early rising must have been of the greatest service to him. He valued the quiet of the early morning hours, when he could seat himself at his clavier and improvise until an idea struck him as being worthy of elaboration. Then he would go about the ordinary work of the day, returning to his idea in the afternoon, elaborating it, giving it form and unity, and only beginning to write when, as he said, he was "quite sure it was the right thing." Thus his handwriting was rapid and clear, and singularly free from corrections. This fact, taken together with the immense number of his compositions, gave rise to the erroneous belief that he composed quickly. This, however, was not the case. His healthy industry and power of abstracting himself from surrounding circumstances were qualities more valuable and telling in the long-run than any mere rapidity of production. When we remember how little of comfort or repose Haydn's home interior afforded, we can but wonder at the power of an art which can raise its follower above the press and wòrry of daily life into the higher and purer region of imagination and creation.

Haydn laid great stress on the importance of melody in music. In his advice to the singer Kelly, whose ambition it was to be thought a composer, he urges upon him that without invention there could be no true genius. The mechanism of composition was of minor importance, and could be perfected by study. "If you want to know whether you have written anything worth preserving," said he, "sing it to yourself without any accompaniment." Master of his art as he was, Haydn would never consent to be bound down by mere rules. Indeed, he often wilfully transgressed in this respect for the sake of producing the effect he intended, and he considered the expression of a new idea of far more importance than the adherence to arbitrary rules. His answer when his attention was drawn to a passage in Mozart's C major quartet showing a disregard of the rules of harmony: "If Mozart wrote it so, he must have had a good reason for it," shows the spirit in which he desired that his own works should be approached.

Haydn's character was so simple and unpretending that envy of other composers, or want of recognition of true merit, wherever it might be found, were feelings which had no place in his mind. His reverence for Ph. Emanuel Bach was that of a disciple, and of Gluck and Handel he always spoke with deep respect. Towards contemporary artists he was generous and appreciative, and the strongest instance of his genuine, and as it were instinctive, admiration for true genius is afforded by the attitude he assumed towards Mozart, while the latter was still a young musician, whom a man of smaller mind might naturally have regarded as a dangerous rival and innovator. "I assure you solemnly," he said to Leopold Mozart, "that I consider your son to be the greatest composer of whom I have ever heard. His taste is excellent, and he has a thorough knowledge of composition." This generous appreciation of others does not by any means imply that Haydn under-estimated his own powers as a composer. "I know," he said to Griesinger as an old man, "that God has bestowed talent upon me, and I humbly acknowledge His goodness in so doing; I think too, I have done my duty in giving to the world the result of my labours; it is for others to follow my example." It is, perhaps, not so singular as might at first sight appear, that Haydn should have set great store by his operatic works, which did not rank high with his contemporaries, and are now virtually forgotten. He says of his "Armida" in March, 1784, that it has been produced with signal success, and is considered his best work, and he writes to his publisher, Artaria (May 27th, 1781) :—

"Mons. Le Gros, Directeur of the Concert Spirituel, writes me many compliments on my Stabat Mater, which has been performed four times with great success. The management were surprised at this revelation of my powers as a vocal composer, but they had had no previous opportunity of judging of them. If they could only hear my operetta, 'L'Isola Disabitata,' and my last opera, 'La Fedeltà Premiata'! I assure you such works have not been heard in Paris, and perhaps not in Vienna; but it is my misfortune to live retired in the country."

Haydn's pecuniary position under Prince Nicolaus was sufficiently good to have enabled him to devote himself to his art with a mind free from anxiety, had not the extravagance and bigotry of his wife brought him into continual difficulties. His salary was about 100*l*. a year, besides his uniform, some allowances in kind, and free quarters for himself and his wife, when she was with him. Three rooms were apportioned to them in the house which was expressly built for the accommodation of the Capelle. Eleven of the musicians had two rooms, and were allowed the company of their wives; the others had but one room, some of them being even lodged two in a room. It is probable that Haydn nearly doubled his salary by the sale of his compositions, in which the prince left him perfectly free. His operas were his least successful works from this point of view. Griesinger says that Haydn had saved about 200*l*. before his journey to London. When we remember his wife's incessant importunity for money, and the calls made upon his resources by his poor relations, calls to which he always made ready response, we can scarcely accept this statement. A less worthy source of expenditure existed during twenty years of Haydn's life in the person of one of the female singers in the Capelle, Luigia Polzelli, who, with her husband, Anton Polzelli, was engaged by Prince Nicolaus in 1779. The vivacious Italian girl (she was only nineteen at the time of her engagement) seems to have completely fascinated Haydn, who was always very susceptible to female influence. Her relations with her husband were no more harmonious than those of Haydn with his wife, and his pity for her soon ripened into a violent affection devoid of any genuine respect or esteem, for which we need the less condemn him since it undoubtedly brought its own punishment, and became the torment of his life for many years. Mdme. Polzelli was a heartless coquette. She turned Haydn's affection to account by continually extorting money from him, and actually induced him, after the death of her husband, to sign a paper promising to marry her, should he become a widower. This, however, he had strength of mind enough to repudiate, and his eyes being at length opened to her true character, his affection for her cooled, the last trace of it being found in his bequest to her of a small annuity. Before Haydn's death she married a singer, Luigi Franchi by name, and died at Kaschau in 1832, at eighty-two years of age.

Now that we have gathered a general idea of Haydn's manner of life and surroundings during the quarter of a century which comprised the most fruitful and progressive years of his musical career, it will be necessary to pass briefly in review the more important of his works between 1766 and 1790, the date of his first visit to London. In doing so we must remember, however, that he is known to the world, especially to the English world of music, principally by his later compositions. His popularity rests on the works of the last twenty years of his life, or what may be called his post-Mozart period, and in estimating his position among musicians we must consider him not as Mozart's predecessor, but as his contemporary and successor. The works which we are about to consider, with the exception of some of the quartets, are now little known and rarely played. They form, nevertheless, a strong foundation for his after-fame, and would repay a far closer examination than we can give as showing how gradually, and as it were unconsciously, Haydn revealed himself as the liberator and prophet of instrumental music. Fortunate as he was in possessing the admiration and confidence of his prince, and of those musicians with whom he was in immediate contact, he did not escape the envy and detraction which fall to the share of all who leave the beaten track to follow their own path. The Viennese public enjoyed his fresh and genial creations with unbounded delight; but the artists and connoisseurs found grave faults with them. The dispute as to whether and in what degree humour could be recognized in music raged loud and long around his works, and the freedom with which he treated conventional rules was found unpardonable by the Vienna critics. His very position with Prince Esterhazy and his residence in Hungary caused him to be distrusted as a foreigner, and the example of the Emperor Joseph II., who disliked him and inveighed against the " tricks and nonsense " with which he overlaid his music was widely followed by the supporters of the older school of instrumental music.

Haydn's dramatic works were, as we know, all composed for the festival occasions which, two or three times in every year, broke the monotony of existence at Esterhaz. A mere recital of the visits of distinguished personages, and of the operas and cantatas composed for each, would be both tiresome and unnecessary. It will be more in accordance with our present object to give an account of one such visit and the entertainment provided for it, and let it serve as a type of all the rest. The pure love of pleasure for its own sake, which was a distinguishing characteristic of the Viennese nobility of the last century, is nowhere more strikingly displayed than on such occasions, when two or three days were entirely devoted to feasting and enjoyment, and neither money nor trouble was spared to make the entertainments the most perfect of their kind.

On August 28th, 1777, the Archduke Ferdinand (son of Francis I. and Maria Theresa) with the Archduchess Maria Beatrice arrived at Esterhaz for a visit of three or four days. As they drove from the village of Szeplak to the palace, their carriages were followed by crowds of peasants uttering shouts of welcome, flourishing trumpets and waving flags. At the entrance to the palace the whole of the prince's establishment was drawn up to receive the visitors. The Esterhazy regiment of grenadiers in full uniform, twenty liveried servants, six couriers, six Hungarian foot-soldiers, the prince's body-guard, the Capelle, the huntsmen, all the household officials, six Hungarian and German pages, lined the steps and the entrance hall. Within the porch the guests were welcomed by the Prince and Princess Esterhazy and a large party of Hungarian and Austrian nobility, invited to meet them. After a short rest in their apartments, which had been specially decorated for this visit, the company repaired to the theatre, where a German play was performed. Then followed an illumination of the palace and part of the park, and the evening closed with a banquet. Early on the following morning, hunting music was played under the windows of the guests' apartments, and after a morning spent in viewing the treasures of art and luxury scattered through the palace, a midday banquet was served in the great hall to the higher nobility, in the summer hall to the lower nobility, and in the marionette theatre to the rest of the company. At four in the afternoon they all drove through the park in open carriages, visiting the temples, grottoes, and other wonders there to be seen, and ending their drive at the theatre, where an opera, "L'Incontro Improvviso," composed by Haydn for the occasion, was performed with much applause. Then came supper, and after that a masked ball, attended by about 1400 guests. On the next day, after dinner, the company walked in the park, and were conducted, accompanied by a band of music, to an open space, where a mimic country fair had been arranged for their amusement, with stalls and booths, mountebanks, quack-doctors, cheap-jacks, puppet-shows, singers and dancers, all in full swing of noise and merriment. After fully enjoying this not over-refined entertainment, the aristocratic guests were served with refreshments and betook themselves to the marionette theatre, where a parody of Gluck's "Alceste" was given, after which came fireworks, supper, and a second ball. The following morning was devoted to the chase; the afternoon to a concert by the Capelle. Then a German comedy was played in the theatre by a Viennese company of actors, and after this and supper the guests were conducted to a cleared space in the park, hung with garlands and planted with rare exotics. A gun was fired, and at the signal the space was filled by a crowd of the prince's peasant subjects in national costume, who, with joyous shouts and songs, danced Hungarian and Croatian dances to national music. When they were tired of looking on, the guests, leaving the peasantry to carry their feasting and dancing far into the night, returned through the park, all hung with coloured lamps, to the palace, where the final banquet and ball were given. Early next morning they took their departure, leaving costly presents in memory of their visit for the performers and officers of the prince's household. Similar entertainments were given in honour of Prince Rohan, French Ambassador extraordinary, in 1772; of the Empress Maria Theresa, in 1773; and on all the other numerous occasions when Esterhaz was visited by royal or distinguished guests. When Haydn was presented to the empress during her visit to Esterhaz, he ventured to remind her Majesty of the "good hiding" he had received at her command long ago at Schönbrunn, and was answered by the good-natured remark, "Well, my dear Haydn, the hiding has borne good fruit, you see."

In July, 1777, at the request of the empress, the Esterhazy Capelle went in a body to Vienna. The occasion was the visit to the Court of Vienna of the Elector of Treves and his sister the Duchess of Saxony, and of the Duke and Duchess of Saxe-Teschen. The performances of the Esterhazy musicians were among the chief of the many costly entertainments given in honour of the royal guests. Two operas during the week, and daily concerts, for which he composed at least one new symphony, can have left Haydn very little leisure for his usual Vienna enjoyments; and besides these a marionette theatre had been specially erected at Schönbrunn for the performance of a marionette opera, probably "Dido," which had been previously produced at Esterhaz at a cost of 6000 florins (about 600*l*.), and which the empress expressed a great desire to see. This visit to Vienna was made while Haydn was still smarting under the failure of his opera, "La Vera Costanza," which he had been commissioned by the court to write for the new Italian Opera in 1777. The strength of his opponents among the musicians and critics was too great for him. and even an appeal to the emperor was of no avail. Haydn withdrew the opera and reproduced it at Esterhaz in 1779.

About this time Haydn sought admission into the Society of Musicians of Vienna, for whose benefit he had already (1775) composed his first oratorio, "Il Ritorno di Tobia." The society, with short-sighted rapacity, not only exacted a sum of 300 florins on account of Haydn's non-residence in the capital, but wished to bind him down to compose for them whenever and whatever they chose to demand. This he at once declared to be incompatible with his duty to Prince Esterhazy, and withdrew his application for membership. Some years later, the society requested him to rearrange his "Tobia" for a fresh performance, but on his stipulating for a payment of 200 florins, they again, with incredible meanness, refused his request, and Hasse's "Elena" was performed instead. Haydn's day of triumph came at last, but not until his second visit to London, when all Europe had hailed him as the greatest musician of his age. Then he received an ovation at a special meeting of the society, and was unanimously appointed "Assessor Senior" for life. He proceeded to heap coals of fire on the society's head, by presenting it with the "Creation" and the "Seasons," and thereby laying the foundation of its after prosperity. Haydn found earlier and more generous appreciation in other countries. The Philharmonic Society of Modena elected him a member in 1780, and in return for this honour he presented the society with his dramatic cantata, "L'Isola Disabitata," performed at Vienna in 1785. In 1784, Prince Henry of Prussia, in return for six quartets dedicated to him, sent Haydn a gold medal and his portrait; and in 1787, King Frederick William II. presented him with a diamond ring in recognition of his merit as a composer. He had just written his cantata, "Germany's Lament on the Death of Frederick the Great." Haydn valued this present exceedingly, and always wore the ring when he was composing anything requiring special pains. A stronger instance of his wide-spread reputation even while he was still confined at Esterhaz, was the commission he received in 1785 to compose the "Seven Last Words of Christ" for the Cathedral of Cadiz. This work Haydn himself esteemed as among the best he had ever composed, and it may interest our readers to have his own account of the circumstances of its performance as prefixed to the edition of the score published by Breitkopf and Härtel in 1801. He writes:—

"About fifteen years ago I was requested by a canon of Cadiz to compose instrumental music on the Seven Words of Jesus on the Cross. It was the custom at the Cathedral of Cadiz to produce an oratorio every year during Lent, the effect of the performance being not a little enhanced by the following circumstances. The walls, windows, and pillars of the church were hung with black cloth, and only one large lamp, hanging from the centre of the roof, broke the solemn obscurity. At midday the doors were closed and the ceremony began. After a short service the bishop ascended the pulpit, pronounced one of the seven words (or sentences) and delivered a discourse thereon. This ended, he left the pulpit and knelt prostrate before the altar. The pause was filled by the music. The bishop then in like manner pronounced the second word, then the third, and so on, the orchestra falling in at the conclusion of each discourse. My composition was to be subject to these conditions, and it was no easy matter to compose seven adagios to last ten minutes each, and follow one after the other without fatiguing the listeners; indeed, I found it quite impossible to confine myself within the appointed limits."

He solved the difficulty by making each instrumental interlude expressive of the words that had preceded it, so that in after-years he was able, by adding words to the music, and dividing it into choruses and solos, to produce it as a sacred cantata. The work made a great impression, and was very often performed.

Haydn's church music has often been characterized as wanting in depth and dignity, and calculated to excite and elate the worshippers, rather than to rouse in them feelings of devotion and contrition. This very fact may account for its wide-spread popularity, so that to this day Haydn's masses and offertories are more frequently performed in Germany than any others. For no one can be unconscious that, underlying the cheerful, almost joyous spirit of his sacred music, is a vein of piety which seeks rather to glorify God's goodness than to deprecate His vengeance, and which encourages the sinner to hope when others might bid him despair. "God has given me a cheerful heart," said Haydn to Carpani, "so He will surely forgive me if I serve Him cheerfully;" and the spirit in which he composed his sacred music shows itself in his simple assertion, that when composing the "Creation," he knelt down every day and prayed to God to give him strength for his work. Between 1766 and 1790 he composed eight masses, besides those sacred compositions we have already noticed and many smaller works. Of the masses the most celebrated is the "Mariazell" Mass in C major, composed for a certain Herr von Kreutzner, apparently as a thanksgiving for his elevation to the rank of a nobleman. This is the only mass Haydn ever wrote to order or for an outside church, and he may well have taken particular pains with it, looking back on his boyish attempt to propitiate the choirmaster at Mariazell, and the curt reception he then met with. The "Cecilia" Mass, in C major, is the longest and most difficult of these masses, and is now only performed in an abridged form.

Haydn's progress as a composer is very strikingly exhibited in the sixty-three symphonies which fall within the period we are considering. The greater number of them are in his earlier style, evidently written to order, and only here and there containing movements of greater depth and originality. As he becomes conscious of his true mission and of its recognition by the world outside his narrow sphere, his hand strengthens, his horizon enlarges, and depth and earnestness become the rule, weak movements the exception. Not yet, however, has he reached the true level of his greatness, and between the best of these symphonies and those written for his London concerts, there is still the difference between endeavour and achievement.

Our space will not allow of our entering upon any detailed account of the symphonies, nor of the occasions for which they were composed, but a word must be given to that cleverest of musical *jeux d'esprit*, the "Farewell" Symphony, the object of which was to persuade the prince to shorten his stay at Esterhaz, and allow his musicians to rejoin their wives and children. We have already seen what a hardship the long separations became, and the Capelle, at last driven to revolt, appealed to Haydn to find a way of making their complaint known without running the risk of incurring the prince's serious displeasure. Haydn pondered the matter over, and the result was that the sixteen members of the Capelle assembled one evening to perform for the first time a symphony by Capellmeister Haydn. Up to the last movement all went well, but in the middle of the finale came a pause—two of the performers quietly packed up their instruments, blew out their candles, and walked out of the orchestra. A few bars further they were followed by another couple, and so it went on until none were left in the orchestra but Tomasini, the prince's prime favourite, and Haydn. At last Tomasini blew out his light and disappeared, and Haydn was in the act of following, when the prince, who had been gazing bewildered at the unexpected performance, stepped forward, and seizing him by the hand, exclaimed, "I see what you mean! They want to go home—very well then—to-morrow we will all be off." We may imagine the anxiety with which Haydn's appearance was waited for in the musician's antechamber, and the jubilation with which his report of the success of the experiment was received. The "Toy" Symphony was doubtless suggested by the medley of noises heard at a village fair. Indeed, Haydn is said to have bought the toy instruments at the fair, and, bringing them home, to have arranged the music for them, supporting them with two violins and a bass. He kept the whole thing a secret from his orchestra, whose merriment at the novel parts they were called upon to take must seriously have retarded the progress of the rehearsal, to which they had been summoned as usual.

Haydn's quartets, of which he wrote upwards of forty during his residence at Esterhaz, were still the most individual expression of his musical genius, and on them he concentrated all the best results of his talent, study, and experience in composition. The estimation in which they were held by those of his contemporaries who were too generous to envy his greatness, is shown by Mozart's affectionate dedication of his first six quartets to Haydn, a compliment he declared to be only his duty, since it was from Haydn that he had learnt how quartets should be written. Haydn's influence, too, is plainly traceable in many of Beethoven's quartets. The lapse of a hundred years has but served to establish Haydn's claim to be considered as the creator of modern chamber music, as surely as his symphonies entitle him to be called the father of the modern orchestra, and we appreciate the vitality of his works the more, remembering the long list of highly esteemed contemporary composers, of whom nothing now remains but their names.

In the clavier music of this period we still find traces

of Emanuel Bach's influence; we know, too, that Haydn had become acquainted with Clementi's works, although it is not likely that his study of them was deep enough to have any marked effect on his own. In any case, he very soon outstripped his forerunners, and became a model of clearness, precision, and judgment to all succeeding composers. His sonatas (twenty-eight are known to belong to this period) still serve as the best foundation for a thorough study of the instrument for which they were written, immensely as this has improved since Haydn's time; and the charm of melody, the consciousness of power, the delight in creating which run through them, captivate the student in spite of himself, and give the works a vitality which bids fair to be immortal. The same may be said of the clavier trios, of which seventeen belong to the Esterhaz period; they, like the sonatas, were composed for the most part for pupils, friends, and special occasions, and still remain models of composition and treatment of melody.

It was not until after 1780 that Haydn first began to compose songs, and the twenty-four included in the first collection are far inferior to those of later years. His literary knowledge was not extensive, and he left the choice of the words to be set to others, the result being often an unfortunate one. His three and four-part songs and his canons were on a higher level, and the latter especially were among his most favourite compositions.

Before closing our account of Haydn's life and works at Esterhaz, we must say a few words on his entry into the order of Freemasons, and that principally because it will lead us to speak of his friendship with Mozart—one of the most genuinely beautiful features in the lives of both these great artists. It was probably at Leopold Mozart's instigation, and while he was visiting his son in Vienna in 1785, that Haydn joined the order; whether it gave him the entry into the select circle for which he hoped, or whether it had any definite effect upon his mental development, we do not know. The most important result of the step was undoubtedly the strengthening of his intimacy with Mozart, himself an ardent Freemason. Haydn's generous acknowledgment of Mozart's merit as a composer has already been alluded to; instances of it occur again and again in his letters and conversation. When it was proposed to produce an opera by Haydn at Prague, together with "Figaro" and "Don Giovanni," he refused to run the risk of putting himself in competition with Mozart, and ended a long eulogy on his brother artist with the words, "Pardon my wandering from the subject—Mozart is a man very dear to me." This was in December, 1787, and in the year following, when controversy was rife in Vienna on the subject of "Don Giovanni," Haydn was one evening appealed to among a large company on some point connected with the opera. "I cannot decide the question in dispute," said he, "but this I know, that Mozart is the greatest composer in the world." Even where they might justly have been considered as rivals, Haydn gave way to the younger man, and declared that if Mozart had written nothing but his violin quartets and the "Requiem," he would have sufficient claim to immortality. He used to declare that he had never heard one of Mozart's compositions without learning something from it, and in 1790 he writes from his solitude at "Estoras," that the north wind had waked him from a dream of listening to the "Nozze di Figaro." The personal intercourse between the two was like that of father and son, and their use to each other of the pronoun *du* was then sufficiently remarkable to be observed by more than one biographer. Mozart felt deeply the separation from his friend when the latter undertook his journey to London, and tried in vain to induce him to give it up, urging his age, ignorance of the world, and want of acquaintance with foreign languages. Haydn replied that he was old certainly (he was fifty-nine), but strong and of good courage, and that his language was understood of all the world. Mozart spent the day of his departure with him, and bade him farewell with tears, saying, "We shall see each other no more in this world!" a presentiment only too sadly to be fulfilled. When the news of Mozart's death reached London, Haydn lamented it with many tears, and wrote to one of his friends (December 20th, 1791) that his only regret in returning home was that he should miss the greeting of the great Mozart. With this pleasant picture, as rare, alas! as it was pleasant in the art world of Vienna in those days, we close our account of Haydn at Esterhaz.

CHAPTER VI.

FIRST VISIT TO LONDON.

1790—1792.

EARLY in 1790, Haydn paid a somewhat longer visit than usual to Vïenna, and his letters written to his friend Frau von Genzinger after his return to the "dreary solitude" of Esterhaz, show plainly enough that his isolated position there was becoming more and more irksome to him. He had already had many pressing invitations to visit foreign countries. The King of Naples was an ardent admirer of his music, and had been so urgent upon him to go to Naples in 1787, that Haydn had almost consented. Le Gros, conductor of the Concerts Spirituels in Paris, wrote to him in 1781, telling him of the enthusiasm with which his Stabat Mater had been received in the French capital, and promising him a brilliant reception if he would visit Paris. But it was in London, perhaps, of all foreign capitals, that Haydn's works found most wide-spread popularity, and the London impresarii, and leaders of the musical world seem to have made up their minds long before he left Esterhaz that sooner or later they would secure his services and his presence among them. W. Cramer, the violinist, wrote to him in 1781, offering to engage him at any cost for the Professional Concerts, and Gallini, owner and manager of the King's Theatre in Drury Lane, pressed him to write an opera for him. Salomon, the most enterprising and energetic of them all, went still further, and in November, 1789, despatched Bland, the well-known music publisher, ostensibly to arrange for the purchase of some new compositions by Haydn, but in reality to try whether personal influence would induce him to leave his post for a wider field of renown. Bland failed, however. Haydn's discontent and chafing sense of servitude always evaporated when he was offered the alternative of leaving his well-loved prince. "My dearest wish is to live and die with him," he wrote in 1776, and not by any act or word of his did he ever show that he wavered in his fidelity. He gave Bland the copyright of several of his compositions, among them the Stabat Mater and "Ariadne" (a cantata for a single voice, with clavier accompaniment, composed in 1782), also the "Razirmesser" (razor) Quartet, which is said to have gained its title from a muttered exclamation of Haydn's while shaving one morning: "I would give my best quartet for a good razor!" Bland, who happened to be entering the room at the moment, immediately ran back to his lodging, and returning with his own razors of good English steel, presented them to Haydn, who gave him in exchange his latest quartet (Trautwein, No. 2.)

As far as the main object of his visit was concerned, however, Bland returned to London only to report failure.

Fortunately for the world, and music, Haydn's devotion was not destined to be put to a much longer test. On the 28th of September, 1790, in the seventy-sixth year of his age, Prince Nicolaus died at Vienna, after a short illness. He had been in a despondent state ever since the death of his wife in February of the same year, and it is affecting to see from Haydn's letters to Frau v. Genzinger with what delicate and affectionate tact he chose such compositions for performance as would not awaken sad memories, but would cheer his bereaved master, by turning his thoughts from his loss. We may be sure that that master himself was mourned with sincere sorrow. He marked his sense of the faithful services of his Capellmeister by leaving him an annual pension of 1000 florins, on condition that he retained the title of Capellmeister to the Esterhazys. The prince doubtless foresaw, what was actually the case, that the Capelle would be disbanded by his successor, Prince Anton, who had no taste for music, and preferred spending his wealth in other ways. He retained in his service only the wind band to perform at banquets, &c., but behaved not ungenerously to the dismissed musicians, adding 400 florins to the pensions of both Haydn and Tomasini.

At last, then, Haydn was free to turn his steps whither he would, certain of welcome and honour wherever his works were known, and secure from all anxiety as to the support of his old age. A residence in Vienna and unrestrained intercourse with his brother artists there, had far more attractions for him than a journey in search of wider fame, and in Vienna he accordingly took up his abode in the quiet household of his old friend Johann Nepomuk Bamberger. He had scarcely had time to realize the fact that he was his own master, when he received an urgent invitation to enter the service of Count Grassalcovics as Capellmeister. This he declined, but had no sooner done so than his tranquillity was again assailed, and this time in a way from which there was no escape. As he sat at work one morning, a strange visitor was announced, who introduced himself in the words, "My name is Salomon. I have come from London to fetch you; we will settle terms to-morrow." He went on to tell Haydn how, on his journey back from Italy, where he had been engaging singers for the Italian Opera in London, he had heard of the death of Prince Nicolaus, and at once hastened to Vienna, resolved this time to take no denial of his long cherished wish to introduce Haydn to the London public. Salomon was the most enterprising and successful *entrepreneur* of his day. He was a native of Bonn, where he was early known as a violin player, and after a short engagement as Concertmeister to Prince Henry of Prussia, he travelled to Paris, and thence to London, where he gradually made himself famous as a performer and conductor, and at last even ventured to announce subscription concerts to rival the Professional Concerts. The years of his greatest prosperity were from 1789 to 1796, when he was director of the Academy of Ancient Music, and his engagement of

Haydn was a master-stroke of musical enterprise for those days, showing him to have been worthy of the position he had gained.

The "coming to terms" was not quite so simple as might at first sight appear. Haydn's doubts, and those of his friends, as to the wisdom of undertaking such a journey at an advanced age had to be overcome; the consent of Prince Anton, whose servant he still was in name, had to be obtained; and the various compositions he had in hand, notably some for the King of Naples, who was then in Vienna, must be finished before he could leave. At last, however, all was arranged. Salomon promised to pay Haydn for one season: 300*l*. for an opera for Gallini; 300*l*. for six symphonies, and 200*l*. more for the copyright of them; 200*l*. for twenty new compositions to be produced by Haydn himself at the same number of concerts; and 200*l*. guaranteed proceeds of a benefit concert. His travelling expenses were paid by Haydn himself, out of his savings, with the addition of 450 florins advanced by the prince. He had also to provide for the maintenance of his wife during his absence, and to assist in this he sold his house at Eisenstadt, which had been the gift of Prince Nicolaus, and had been twice rebuilt after being destroyed by fire. On the 8th of December, Salomon wrote to London to John Baptist Mara, husband of the celebrated singer, and musical critic of the *St. James's Chronicle*, requesting him to insert in that journal a notice of Haydn's projected visit to London. The notice appeared on the 30th of December, and informed the public that immediately on his arrival with his distinguished guest, Mr. Salomon would have the honour of submitting to all lovers of music his programme for a series of subscription concerts, the success of which would depend upon their support and approbation.

Two days before leaving Vienna, Haydn, after long delay, secured an audience with the King of Naples, and presented the compositions (seven notturni for two lyres) which he had been commissioned to write. "Good!" said the king, "we will rehearse them the day after to-morrow."

"The day after to-morrow," replied Haydn, "I shall be on my way to England." "What!" cried the king; "and you had promised to come to me in Naples!" and he left the room angrily. Haydn waited a little, uncertain whether to go or stay. In a short time the king returned, having recovered from his ill-humour, and gave Haydn a letter of introduction to the Neapolitan Ambassador in London, with the request that at least he would visit Naples on his return from England. He also sent him the same evening a valuable gold snuff-box in return for his compositions.

On the evening of the 15th of December, 1790, Haydn and Salomon left Vienna. They journeyed by way of Munich to Bonn, where they arrived on Christmas Day. Salomon's visit to his native place, accompanied by so distinguished a guest, could not fail to create a considerable sensation, especially as Bonn was then the residence of the Elector of Cologne, Archbishop Maximilian Francis, the youngest son of Maria Theresa, who had inherited a full share of the family talent for music. On Sunday, December 26th, Salomon took Haydn to hear mass sung by the Elector's Capelle, one of the best in Europe. To his great gratification one of his own masses was performed, and after the service he was summoned to the "Oratorium," where he found the Elector, who received him with a graceful compliment, and presented him to the principal members of the Capelle. From Bonn the travellers proceeded to Brussels, and thence to Calais, where they arrived in heavy rain on the evening of the last day of the year. The following morning at half-past seven they embarked for Dover, but were tossed about by contrary winds for several hours, not setting foot on English ground until five in the afternoon. Haydn rejoiced to make his first acquaintance with the sea, and remained on deck during the whole voyage. But he acknowledges to having felt "a little frightened, and a little uncomfortable" as the wind rose, most of the passengers being very sea-sick and "looking like ghosts."

It may be as well here to mention that almost all our information concerning Haydn's impressions and opinions of England and the English during his first visit to London is derived from his letters to Frau von Genzinger, which were collected and published, with an introductory account of the circumstances of his visit by Herr von Karajan, in 1861. The letters are otherwise interesting, as showing the pure and elevating friendship which existed between Haydn and this amiable and highly cultivated woman, a friendship which stands in happy contrast to his relations with Mdme. Polzelli.

Haydn's first two days in London were devoted to recovering from the effects of his journey, which had no doubt been a strange and fatiguing experience to one who had led so quiet and uneventful a life. But he soon began to look about him, and his shrewd, observant mind took in the main characteristics of people and place with astonishing rapidity. His first night was passed under the roof of Bland, the music publisher, at 45, High Holborn, but on the following day Salomon made arrangements for his lodging in the same house with himself, 18, Great Pulteney Street, Golden Square. Haydn calls it, "a nice, convenient lodging, but very dear," and praises the cooking, the landlord being an Italian cook. His first impression seems to have been of the size of London, which appeared to him enormous, even in those days, before Regent Street was built, and when Lisson Grove was a country lane, to which he afterwards retreated in search of quiet. Then the noise, especially the multitude of discordant street cries, oppressed him greatly, and must have caused him many a time to sigh over his work for the sylvan repose of Esterhaz, or for the quiet of his little study in Vienna. The hospitality with which he was received gratified him extremely, and he writes to Frau v. Genzinger that his presence in London having been announced in all the newspapers within three days of his arrival, he had received most flattering attentions from the nobility, had visited, and received visits from the Austrian and Neapolitan Ambassadors, and had dined out six times in seven days. But he goes on to lament the late hour (six o'clock) at which dinner-parties were given in London, and resolves to decline future invitations on account of his health, and to dine at home with Salomon at four o'clock. He refused also to receive visitors before two in the afternoon, devoting his mornings to work. He soon gauged the musical taste of the English public, and rearranged most of his compositions written earlier, before producing them in London. Our national manners in the concert-room would seem to have descended to us from our grandfathers, for we find Haydn doubting as to which of two evils he shall choose; whether to insist on his stipulated composition being placed in the first or the second part of each concert's programme. In the former case, its effect would be marred by the continual noisy entrance of late comers; while in the latter case, a considerable portion of the audience would probably be asleep before it began. Haydn chose this, however, as the preferable alternative, and the loud chord (Paukenschlag) of the andante in the "Surprise" Symphony is said to have been the comical device he hit upon for rousing the slumberers.

In spite of his determination to secure tranquillity for steady work, Haydn found his time taken up in receiving the visits of all the principal musical celebrities then in London, and in a multitude of social engagements from which there was no escape. In his old friend Gyrowetz he was glad to greet a familiar face in a foreign land, and he was pleased also to become personally acquainted with the greatest authority of the English musical world, Dr. Burney, with whom he had already corresponded for several years. Burney mentions Haydn's arrival in his diary as a blessing to the lovers of music, for which they have to thank Salomon, and he celebrated the event in a poem which appeared in the *Monthly Review*, the last stanza of which we reproduce, as an example of the literary homage of the day.

> Welcome, great master! to our favoured isle,
> Already partial to thy name and style;
> Long may thy fountain of invention run
> In streams as rapid as it first begun;
> While skill for each fantastic whim provides,
> And certain science ev'ry current guides!

Oh, may thy days, from human suff'rings free,
Be blest with glory and felicity,
With full fruition, to a distant hour,
Of all thy magic and creative pow'r!
Blest in thyself, with rectitude of mind,
And blessing, with thy talents, all mankind!

The Salomon subscription concerts were announced to take place on the 11th of February and every succeeding Friday, the subscription for the series of twelve being five guineas. Haydn was under contract to supply a new composition for each evening, and the list of singers contained names which it was hoped would enable the enterprise to compete successfully with the professional concerts. In the meantime Haydn was the object of admiring homage wherever he went. At the concert given by the Academy of Ancient Music in the Freemasons' Hall on the 6th of January, the whole audience applauded vehemently as he walked up the middle of the hall to the orchestra, and at the conclusion of the performance he was conducted into the banqueting-room, where covers were laid for 200 musical amateurs, the place of honour being reserved for Haydn. He excused himself, however, from remaining longer than was necessary to drink to the health of those present in a bumper of Burgundy. On the 12th of January he attended the meeting of the Anacreontic Society at the "Crown and Anchor," in the Strand. Here, again, he was received with every demonstration of respect and admiration, and expressed much pleasure at the manner in which one of his own symphonies was performed by the orchestra. On the 18th of January the Queen's birthday was celebrated by the usual firing of cannons, decking of ships on the river, and by a drawing-room, where the Prince of Wales appeared wearing 80,000*l*. worth of diamonds. In the evening there was a court ball, to which Haydn was invited—an unprecedented honour, since he had not yet been presented at court. He was flatteringly noticed by the Prince of Wales, and was the object of attention from all present. On the very next evening we find him taking part in a concert at Carlton House, and on the

2nd of February he was present at the first Ancient Music Concert for the season (their Majesties' concerts), given in the hall in Tottenham Street, now the Prince of Wales's Theatre. These concerts were the most classical and select of any in London, owing much of their success to the constant and active patronage of the royal family. Their fundamental rule, confining the performances to the works of musicians who had been dead twenty years, fettered the action of the management considerably, and the royal interference did not tend to introduce a more liberal spirit. On the present occasion, for instance, Handel being still the reigning deity at court, fifteen out of the eighteen pieces were by him, Corelli, Jomelli, and Graun being each represented by one. It was Haydn's great desire that one of his compositions should be performed at an Ancient Music Concert. But the management steadily refused to make any exception to their rule, and it was not until forty-one years later that—the allotted twenty years of posthumous fame being fulfilled—this conservative body announced a work of Haydn's ("Let there be Light," from the "Creation") for performance at one of their concerts.

In the meantime, Salomon had found himself obliged to postpone his first concert, Cappelletti and David, the two principal vocalists engaged, being under contract not to sing in public before the opening of the new Opera House in the Haymarket, an event which met with so much opposition that there was some doubt at last whether it would take place at all. The first postponement was to February 25th, but the contest between Gallini and his opponents who supported the Pantheon and declared the opening of a second Italian Opera House undesirable, was then at its height, and a further postponement was necessary. The concert was finally fixed for the 11th of March, and permission was given to David to appear whether the Opera House was open or not. The delay seemed likely to prove most injurious to Haydn's interests. It allowed Salomon's opponents, the directors of the Professional Concerts, to gain the start of him, and gave them the ear of the public before Haydn had had an opportunity of justifying the pretensions with which he had entered on his London season. The public ardour was cooled by depreciatory paragraphs in the newspapers, sneering at the composer as a nine days' wonder, whom closer acquaintance would prove to be inferior to either Cramer or Clementi; and alluding to the "proverbial avarice" of the Germans as tempting so many artists who met with scanty recognition from their own countrymen to herald their arrival in England with such a flourish of trumpets as should charm the money out of the pockets of easily-gulled John Bull.

The first Professional Concert took place on the 7th of February, and their jealousy of Haydn, or, more truly, their mortification at not having succeeded in securing his services for themselves, did not prevent the directors including in their programme two of his compositions, a quartet and a MS. symphony. They even went so far as to present him with a free ticket of admission to the whole series of concerts, an attention which Haydn, who throughout seems to have been in a great measure unconscious of the strength of their opposition, received with great gratification. He also declared that he had never heard his symphony so well performed.

On the 18th of February, Haydn's "Ariadne a Naxos" (the cantata for solo voice, with piano accompaniment, already mentioned, p. 81), was sung by Signor Pacchierotti, accompanied by Haydn himself, at one of the ladies' concerts in the house of Mrs. Blair, of Portland Place. This composition was a favourite with Haydn, and became very popular in London. The *Morning Chronicle* of the 23rd of February calls it, in a somewhat rhapsodical notice of the concert, "the musical desideratum for the season." It was repeated at the concert of the new Musical Fund a week later, and his performance of it added greatly to Pacchierotti's reputation as a vocalist.

Meantime, Haydn was carefully rehearsing the symphony for his first concert, on which so much depended, and an anecdote told by Dies is worth repeating here as an illustration of his demeanour towards his orchestra. The symphony opens as usual with a short adagio beginning with three single notes. The orchestra played these much too loud, and Haydn stopped them with a "St! st!" and a request, which Salomon interpreted, that they would try again. The second attempt, however, and even a third were no more successful, and Haydn was beginning to grow impatient, when he overheard one of the musicians, a German, say to another in his own language, " I say, if the first three notes don't please him, how shall we get through all the rest?" Haydn thereupon checked himself, and explained to the orchestra with great politeness that he regretted very much not understanding their language, but that the favour he asked of them was quite within their power, as he would soon show if one of them would be so kind as to lend him an instrument. Then, taking a violin, he played the three notes so that the orchestra at once understood and acted upon his wishes. His invariable habit, in London as in Esterhaz, was to coax rather than to frighten his musicians into obeying him, but we can imagine him many a time sighing for his "liebe Kinder" at home, who understood his every gesture, and had learned to interpret his works as though they were their own.

At last the 11th of March arrived, and the first of the Salomon-Haydn concerts took place. The reality of Haydn's popularity was put to the test, and the result was an unquestionable success. Hanover Square Rooms, at that time the principal concert-hall in London, was filled with a brilliant and intelligent audience. Salomon led the orchestra as first violin, and Haydn presided at the pianoforte. In these days of giant effects, we may smile at the appointments of Salomon's orchestra, but it was then considered exceptionally strong. It contained sixteen violins, four tenors, three violoncelli, four double basses, flutes, oboes, bassoons, horns, trumpets, and drums, in all about forty performers. The principal vocalists were Mdme. Storace and Signor David. Mdme. Gautherot, a favourite with the London public, before whom she first appeared in 1789, was the solo violinist, and Dussek accompanied Mdme. Krumpholz in a duet of his own composition for piano and harp. Burney tells us that

Haydn's appearance in the orchestra seemed to have an electrical effect on all present, and he never remembered a performance where greater enthusiasm was displayed. Haydn's symphony was the second of the Salomon symphonies. It was received with great applause, and the adagio was encored, an event of so unusual occurrence that Haydn remembered to tell it years after to Griesinger, as a thing to be noted in his biography. Dr. Pohl ("Haydn in London," p. 121) remarks on the enthusiasm for good music existing in the smaller London of a century ago, as proved by the fact that on the evening of Haydn's first concert, crowded audiences attended oratorio performances both in Covent Garden and in Drury Lane theatres.

A mere enumeration of Haydn's London concerts, with a list of performers more or less forgotten or unknown to the general reader of to-day, would serve only to weary and confuse, and would answer our present purpose less than a more comprehensive view of his social life and doings during his stay in England. The success of the first concert was maintained throughout the series. The Prince of Wales was present at the second, when, "by special desire," the symphony already performed was repeated. At the third, a new cantata by Haydn was sung by Mdme. Storace.

In the meantime, the faction fight round the opening of Gallini's new theatre raged fiercer and fiercer. The building was on a far larger scale than the old one it replaced. As composers, Gallini had secured Haydn and Federici, and his list of singers and ballet composed a brilliant company, Salomon being leader of the orchestra. One thing only was wanting—the Lord Chamberlain's licence, without which no operatic or dramatic performance could be given. The management of the Pantheon raised heaven and earth to prevent the establishment of a rival theatre. The contest spread to newspapers, public meetings, and even to families. The court took opposite sides, as Horace Walpole writes to Miss Agnes Berry (Feb. 18, 1791), "The rival theatre is said to be magnificent and lofty, but it is doubtful whether it will be suffered to come to light; in short, the contest will grow political, 'Dieu et mon droit' (the king) supporting the Pantheon, and 'Ich dien' (the Prince of Wales) countenancing the Haymarket. It is unlucky that the amplest receptacle is to hold the minority."

The Pantheon opened on the 17th of February, and a fortnight later, Gallini announced a public dress rehearsal at the new King's Theatre, which on this occasion was crowded with invited guests. They overflowed on to the stage, and interfered with the performance of Mdme. Vestris in the ballet of "Orfeo ed Eurydice." But all was in vain. The decision of the Lord Chamberlain was finally and decidedly given against the opening of a second house for operatic performances. All that Gallini could obtain was a licence for "entertainments" of music and dancing, with which he opened the theatre on the 26th of March. A series of mixed entertainments, half-concert, half-ballet, were given twice a week during the season, and many works by Haydn were there performed. Among them were symphonies, quartets, and other instrumental pieces; also various choruses (including the "Storm" to Peter Pindar's words, "Hark, the wild uproar of the waves"), and a cantata, specially composed for Signor David, and accompanied by Haydn himself. The opera, "Orfeo," which he had been commissioned before leaving Vienna to prepare for the new theatre, had of course to be abandoned, and knowing how he had all his life longed to be recognized as an operatic composer, we cannot but sympathize in his disappointment. While he was working at it, and still hoping for its performance, he retired for quiet and seclusion to Lisson Grove, scarcely a spot one would choose with such an object now-a-days! It was fortunate for Haydn that the agreement as to the payment for the opera had been signed before he left Vienna. He took the unfinished work back with him, and, by way of compensation, sent to London the autograph score of his "Armida" (composed in 1783), which is now in the library of the Sacred Harmonic Society.

Haydn's benefit concert was given on the 10th of May,

the receipts, guaranteed at 200*l*., amounting to 350*l*. Two grand symphonies were included in the programme, one of them the same that had already been twice played at the Salomon concert, having apparently taken a firm hold on the affections of the public. On the 30th of May a performance of the "Seven Words," composed for Cadiz (p. 73), was given, also for Haydn's benefit, under the title of "La Passione Instrumentale," and excited an amount of enthusiasm which bid fair to rival that caused by the Handel Festival which was taking place during the same week in Westminster Abbey. The "Passione Instrumentale" was performed again on the 10th of June, at the benefit concert of the boy violinist, F. Clement, then ten years old. Haydn conducted the concert, which also included one of his symphonies, a compliment which Clement repaid seventeen years later by taking the first violin at the last concert Haydn ever attended, a performance of the "Creation" at Vienna, on the 27th of March, 1808.

The idea of commemorating the centenary of Handel's birth (1684) by a grand performance of some of his works had originated in 1783 with three musical amateurs, Viscount Fitzwilliam, Sir Watkin Williams Wynn, and Joah Bates, and was supported by the directors of the Ancient Music Concerts, and warmly entered into by George III. Two performances were given in Westminster Abbey in 1784, with a success so unprecedented as to establish beyond doubt Handel's claim to the first place among musicians loved and honoured by the English people. The commemoration of 1784 was followed by others in 1785, 1786, 1787, 1790, and 1791, the sixth and last of the century.

Haydn's presence at the Handel Festival was an important event in his musical career. He had never before heard a performance on so grand a scale, the orchestra and chorus together numbering upwards of 1000 persons. Mdme. Mara, Mrs. Crouch, and Mdme. Storace, Messrs. Pacchierotti, David, and Kelly were among the solo singers, and the principal instrumentalists were the best of the day. A guinea was the price of admission, and an advertisement in the *Gazetteer* announced that "ladies would not be admitted in hats, and were particularly requested to come without feathers, and with very small hoops, if any." Haydn had a good seat close to the king's box, and the beauty and solemnity of the scene and the performance appear to have affected him strongly. When at the Hallelujah Chorus the whole assembly, including the king, rose to their feet, he wept like a child, exclaiming in overpowering emotion, "He is the Master of us all!"[1]

During the first week of July, Haydn attended the Oxford Commemoration, in order that he might receive the honorary degree of Doctor of Music, an honour which he could hardly be expected to understand or care very much about. It was, in fact, due to the suggestion and determined partisanship of Dr. Burney, who no doubt considered it as the crown and summit of all earthly distinctions to be conferred on a musician. Nevertheless, Haydn seems to have been greatly impressed and even somewhat amused by the ceremonies of his installation, and it is much to be regretted that a letter to Frau von Genzinger, describing the affair in detail, has been lost. Among the festivities of the week were three grand concerts, for which all the principal singers and instrumentalists in London were engaged. At the first of these Haydn was led in by Dr. Hayes, Professor of Music at Oxford, and was received "with the honour and attention due to his great and extraordinary talent." He had written a symphony expressly for the occasion, but having arrived in Oxford too late to rehearse it, a better known one was substituted. At the second concert the new symphony, the "Oxford" Symphony as it is called, was performed with great

[1] The custom of rising for the Hallelujah Chorus originated at its first performance in London in 1749, when the audience was so transported by that part of it beginning, "For the Lord God Omnipotent reigneth," that they all, including the king, started to their feet, and remained standing to the end of the chorus. Haydn says in one of his letters that Mdme. Mara was hissed at Oxford because she had failed to rise during a performance of the Hallelujah Chorus.

applause, and Clement's violin playing and David's singing excited immense enthusiasm among the undergraduates. Of the symphony the *Morning Chronicle* of the 11th of July says : " A more wonderful composition never was heard. The applause given to Haydn, who conducted this admirable effort of his genius, was enthusiastic; but the merit of the work, in the opinion of all the musicians present, exceeded all praise." On the following day, the ceremony of conferring the degree took place, and at the third and last concert, given the same evening, Haydn appeared in his doctor's gown, and amid a storm of applause rose, and seizing the gown, raised it as high as he could, exclaiming in English, " I thank you ! " at which the applause redoubled. " I had to walk about for three days in this guise," he writes, " and only wish my Vienna friends could have seen me." In acknowledgment of the honour done to him, Haydn sent the university a three-part canon, afterwards used for the first of the Ten Commandments, the whole of which he set to canons during his stay in London.

Haydn found himself on his return to London the object of still greater attention and admiration than before. His doctor's degree had doubtless some influence in causing him to be sought after and fêted in circles to which he might not otherwise have had access. He appears to have taken the lionizing very simply and as his proper due, and to have enjoyed the river parties and picnics given in his honour more than the lengthy dinners or evening entertainments in town, which must have been particularly trying to a guest who, although the object of universal remark, was unable to express himself in the language of his entertainers, or understand their complimentary observations. Mr. John Taylor, in his amusing " Records of my Life " (London, 1832), gives an account of a dinner at Mdme. Mara's, where the party consisted of Dr. Wolcot (Peter Pindar), Crosdill the violoncellist, Salomon, and Haydn. After dinner Crosdill proposed to celebrate Haydn's presence with three times three. The proposal was warmly adopted all the guests but Haydn standing up and cheering lustily. He, hearing his name, but not understanding what was going on, stared at them with surprise. When it was explained to him by Salomon, he appeared quite overcome with diffidence, putting his hands before his face, and not recovering his equanimity for some minutes.

It was probably early in August that Haydn received a summons from Prince Esterhazy to return to Vienna at once, in order to write an opera for some forthcoming festivities there. He mentions the circumstance in a letter to Frau v. Genzinger, dated September 17th, evidently expecting that the refusal which, in view of the engagements he had entered into for several months to come, he was compelled to give, would cost him his position and pension as Capellmeister to the prince. The latter, however, perhaps hardly expected a more favourable answer, for he seems to have expressed no greater disapprobation than was conveyed in his greeting to Haydn when they met again: "Ah, Haydn! you might have saved me 40,000 florins."

The London season being now quite over, Haydn followed the example of the rest of the world, and left town in search of rest and refreshment. His letter to Frau v. Genzinger last mentioned, is written from the country house of a banker of Lombard Street. Haydn tells his friend how the seclusion ("like a convent," he says) and country air have completely cured his rheumatism, and how he wanders through the woods in the early summer morning, his thoughts straying from the English Grammar he holds in his hand, to his home in Vienna, his family, his friends, and most of all to his best and dearest friends in the Schottenhof. The only personal anecdote preserved of this visit is given by Dies on Haydn's own authority, and must have been accepted by his fellow-countrymen as a striking instance of English "spleen." We cannot but think that good father Haydn was quizzing his faithful Boswell when he gravely related that Herr ———, having begged him to tell the story of his early life, was so much struck by the contrast between the young musician's struggles and privations, and his own unbroken prosperity that, jumping up, he called for pistols, and would have put an end to his existence then and there, had he not been restrained by the tearful solicitations of his wife and family.

Haydn had need of all the refreshment and energy which nature and the hospitality of his friends could bestow. Stormy days awaited his return to town. The "Professionals," more than ever bent on overthrowing Salomon's undertaking, and finding that Haydn had gained too firm a hold on the popular favour to be displaced by any rival they had as yet produced, made repeated and strenuous efforts to win the master himself over to their side, and induce him to abandon Salomon and Gallini. Knowing Haydn's honesty of purpose, and love of upright dealing as we do, we are not surprised to find him firmly rejecting these overtures. "I will not," he says, "break my word to Gallini and Salomon, nor shall any desire for dirty gain induce me to do them an injury. They have run so great a risk, and gone to so much expense on my account, that it is only fair that they should be the gainers by it." Driven to resort to another and, if possible, a still meaner device, the enemy all at once informed the newspaper-reading world that Haydn having become far too old and infirm to produce anything new worth hearing, and having long since come to an end of his musical ideas, and been forced to repeat himself in all that he composed, it had been found necessary to provide for the Professional Concerts a composer of more original genius, who was presented to the public in the person of Herr Ignaz Pleyel, himself the most famous pupil of the worn-out master.

Pleyel had, in fact, taken lessons from Haydn in 1770, and was now Capellmeister at Strasburg. He was in his thirty-fourth year, a clever and conscientious musician, but one who had himself no idea of rivalling the master, to whom he and all his contemporaries looked up as disciples. He must have been astonished at the honour thus suddenly thrust upon him. It does not appear that he had much, if any, knowledge of the intrigues in which he was designed to act as the tool; his whole demeanour towards Haydn from first to last showed the respect and affection due to the older and greater musician. Haydn, better informed than Pleyel as to the true state of affairs, took the most efficient means of defeating his opponents' designs by appearing on the best terms with his rival both in public and private. Curiously enough, Pleyel took lodgings in the same street, exactly opposite Haydn's rooms, and the laconic entries in the diary of the latter for the 23rd of December, "*Pleyel came to London,*" and the 24th., "*I dined with him,*" are sufficiently indicative of the discomfiture which awaited those who strove to make their own profit by pitting one genius against another. We do not say that occasions did not arise when Haydn found it necessary to defend his pretensions against those of his pupil. Dr. John Taylor, whom we have already quoted (p. 95), tells us of an occasion when he dined with Haydn and Salomon at a coffee-house in Vere Street. Dr. Wolcot was again the other guest present, and Salomon, who was an intelligent and observant traveller, entertained the party with anecdotes of various musicians whom he had met in Germany. At length the name of Pleyel was mentioned, and Dr. Wolcot, who was apt to blunder, burst into rapturous praise of his taste and genius as a musician. Haydn listened with ready consent for some time, but at length, as the doctor grew more and more enthusiastic in Pleyel's praises, he remarked with considerable warmth, "But I hope it will be remembered that he was my pupil." The poor doctor, realizing his mistake, stammered forth a confused apology, which Haydn no doubt accepted with a good grace.

On November 5th, Haydn was present at the banquet and ball at Guildhall, given to the outgoing Lord Mayor, and again at the entertainment on the 9th, which concluded the ceremony of Lord Mayor's Day. His diary gives with graphic simplicity his impressions of the heat, the smell of the lamps, the babel of tongues drowning the dance music (fortunately enough, it would seem, for when Haydn did hear it, it was so bad, he beat a hasty retreat), and the conviviality of the male guests, who sat about in the ball-room drinking, singing, waving their glasses,—and shouting "Hurrah!" without intermission all through the night.

An entry in Haydn's diary for November 23rd records a visit to a marionette theatre in Savile Row, which would no doubt interest him by comparison with that of Esterhaz. He thought the figures good, the singers bad, and the orchestra tolerable. On the following day he left London for a three days' visit to Oatlands Park, as the guest of the Duke of York, who was spending his honeymoon there with his young bride, the Princess of Prussia. The sight of the kind German face, and the familiar sound of the German tongue of the musician, whose name had been a household word to her ever since she could speak, must have been more than welcome to the little transplanted bride (she was only seventeen), and Haydn writes tenderly to Frau v. Genzinger (December 20th) how the "liebe Kleine" sat close by his side all the time he was playing his symphony, humming the familiar airs to herself, and urging him to go on playing until long past midnight. Haydn's portrait was painted during this visit, by order of the Prince of Wales. The artist was John Hoppner, R.A., and the picture now hangs in the gallery of Hampton Court. Haydn next paid a visit to Sir Patrick Blake at Langham, stopping on his way at Cambridge, where he was exceedingly interested in all he saw. He remained only three days at Langham, returning to London in time to be present at a performance of Shield's comic opera, "The Woodman," at Covent Garden, on December 10th, with Mrs. Billington as Emily. He writes that she sang "timidly, but very well." The fogs of a London November, or more probably, the chills and fatigue incidental on long and unaccustomed journeys so late in the year, brought on a severe attack of rheumatism, which Haydn expressively characterizes as "English" in its severity, and which obliged him, as he says, to clothe himself from head to foot in flannel, by which means he hopes the enemy will soon be overcome.

But before the year closed a sharper cry of pain was

to escape him than any caused by bodily suffering, however severe. The entry in his diary, "*Mozart died on the 10th December,* 1791," is pathetic in its brevity, and we can well believe that at the moment Haydn could trust himself to write no more than this. In his subsequent letters his grief finds freer vent, and months after, when time had softened the blow, he writes that his pleasure in returning home is embittered by the thought that no Mozart will be there to welcome him.

So ended the year 1791. The musical campaign of 1792 opened with an advantage to the Professionals. They again had the start of Salomon, giving their first concert, on the 13th of February, and showing their diplomacy by treating Haydn with every mark of respect, both personally and as a composer. His name was the first on the programme, and the symphony composed by Pleyel specially for this concert was pretty severely criticized as an instance of presumption on the part of the pupil towards his master. The two musicians, however, continued to be on the most friendly terms, and Salomon repaid the compliment paid to Haydn by the Professionals by putting a symphony by Pleyel at the head of the programme of his first concert, which took place on February 17th. The programme is one of exceptional variety for those days, containing solos for the oboe (Mr. Harrington), and for the harp (Mdme. Delavalle), as well as for the violin (Felix Yaniewicz).[2]

At Salomon's second concert, on the 24th of February, Haydn's "Storm Chorus," which has already been mentioned (p. 92), was performed with the greatest success. Haydn was especially proud of this, his first achievement in setting English words to music. At each of the six concerts of the series some grand composition by Haydn, either vocal or instrumental, was given, and at his benefit concert, on the 3rd of May, every piece in the programme was his, except a violin concerto, composed and played

---

[2] Grandfather of the present writer. He appeared in most of Haydn's subsequent concerts, and always with great applause. His playing was noted for its refinement and expressive delivery. He afterwards settled in Edinburgh.

by Yaniewicz. Haydn twice conducted concerts for other musicians during the spring—once for Barthelemon, the well-known violinist (who had been settled in London for forty-four years, and with whom Haydn formed a very close friendship), and once for Haesler, the pianoforte player and composer. One of the greatest pleasures he enjoyed during his residence in London, was afforded him by the Anniversary Meeting of Charity Children at St. Paul's Cathedral in June of this year. The sight is always one of the most impressive that can be, and the sound of the young voices echoing through the aisles no doubt recalled to Haydn the Cantorei and St. Stephen's, where a little neglected boy had sent out all his heart in the music which was its only language and its only joy.

Haydn's diary mentions his acquaintance with the astronomer William Herschel and his sister as one of great interest to him; but the friend who became more dear to him than almost any other, including even Frau v. Genzinger herself, was Mrs. Schroeter, widow of the queen's music-master, John S. Schroeter. She seems to have been an attractive, although, according to modern taste, a somewhat vulgar woman of over sixty years of age, and there is no disguising the fact that she made violent love to Haydn, and succeeded in inspiring him, on his side, with so much affection for her that he declared he would certainly have married her if he had been free. Her letters to Haydn are full of tenderness, and in questionable taste; his to her have not been preserved, but we can have little doubt that they were warmer in tone than they would have been had not the Channel rolled between him and Frau Haydn in Vienna. It may, indeed, have been some rumour of the affair reaching home which caused that good lady to write and urge his return, mentioning that she had seen a little house which she liked very much, and which would suit her admirably as a residence *during her widowhood*. She begged Haydn at once to send her 2000 gulden, that she might conclude the purchase. He did not accede to this request, but came himself, saw the house, bought it, and lived in it for nine years after his wife's death in the year 1800.

CHAPTER VII.

SECOND VISIT TO LONDON.

1794, 1795.

IN one of Haydn's last letters from London, he reviews his difficulties and triumphs there, and thanks God that he has been enabled to overcome the determined opposition of his enemies, and to retain the favour of the public. "But," he adds, "I must acknowledge that I am tired and worn out with my many labours, and that I look forward with intense longing to my return home to rest." With this feeling he prepared for his journey to Vienna, planning to arrive there at the end of July. He altered his intended route, and gave up a visit to Berlin, where he had been warmly invited by King Frederick William II., in order to meet Prince Anton Esterhazy at Bonn. A meeting here of more interest to us was that with Beethoven, who submitted a cantata to Haydn, which the latter warmly praised, encouraging the young composer to continue his studies, and probably then making arrangements for receiving and instructing him in Vienna, whither the Elector was on the point of sending him. All who know Beethoven's life know that these lessons, which extended over the first year of his residence in Vienna, were practically a failure, and that Haydn's influence on Beethoven, though undoubtedly very great, was the indirect one resulting from the attraction always exerted upon genius by genius, to which Beethoven was perhaps more susceptible than any other composer. In truth, Haydn had grown a little above giving lessons in counterpoint, even to a young Beethoven. His London fame had preceded him to Vienna, and he found himself the idol of society. His time was occupied by engagements of many kinds, and it cannot be denied that he neglected his pupil (he was paid, by the way, about 9½d. an hour for the lessons), who had recourse to Schenk, a well-known composer, for additional instruction. The division between Haydn and Beethoven gradually widened. Haydn abandoned the intention he had once formed of taking the young musician with him to England, and Beethoven, with characteristic impatience and want of tact, refused to call himself Haydn's pupil, and lost no opportunity of making irritating remarks hurtful to the old man's vanity. In after-years these unworthy feelings disappeared, and Beethoven's later sentiments are proved by his exclamation already quoted (p. 41), on being shown a view of Haydn's birthplace.

There is little to be said of Haydn's life in Vienna for the next eighteen months. He took up his abode in the house, situated in the suburb of Gumpendorf, about which his wife had written to him in London. It was quiet and retired, with a little garden round it, and Haydn liked it so well that he bought it, planning the addition of another storey when he should be away in London again. During the summer of 1793 Haydn visited his birthplace, gazed with tender emotion on the spot which was hallowed by the memories of his parents' love, bent down and kissed the threshold their feet had so often crossed, and audibly expressed the gratitude due to them for those lessons of industry and rectitude which had never faded from his mind. The occasion of Haydn's visit to Rohrau was the inauguration of a monument erected in his honour by Count Harrach, in one of the most beautiful glades of his park. It consisted of a square pillar surmounting three stone steps, with an inscription on each side, and supporting a bust of Haydn in marble.

In the winter of this year Haydn produced his six London symphonies at the concerts of the Musicians' Benevolent Society, and the reception accorded to them was most enthusiastic.

Before allowing Haydn to leave London, Salomon had stipulated with him for the composition of six new symphonies, and had made him promise, if possible, to conduct them in person. Accordingly before the year closed Haydn applied to Prince Anton for a second leave of absence, a leave most reluctantly given, and postponed as long as possible, so long indeed, that with all the haste he could make on his journey, Haydn arrived in London the day after that which had been fixed for Salomon's first concert. It was postponed, therefore, from the 3rd to the 10th of February, and before it took place Haydn had the pain of hearing that Prince Anton was no more. He had died three days after Haydn's departure, and was succeeded by his son Nicolaus, who inherited his grandfather's love of music and pride in his celebrated Capellmeister. Haydn was accompanied on his second visit to London by his favourite servant and copyist, Johann Elssler,[1] and took lodgings this time at 1, Bury Street, St. James's, probably in order to be near Mrs. Schroeter. Salomon's rivals, the Professionals, were now no more, and Haydn was left in undisputed possession of the field as the first composer of the day. Their series of twelve

[1] We extract the following from Groves' "Dictionary of Music and Musicians," vol. i. p. 712, note: "The name of Elssler is closely associated with that of Haydn from 1766, the date of Joseph Elssler's marriage at Eisenstadt, at which Haydn assisted. Joseph was a native of Silesia, and music copyist to Prince Esterhazy. His children were taken into the Capelle on Haydn's recommendation, and the second son, Johannes (born at Eisensthat, 1769) lived the whole of his life with him, first as copyist and then as general servant and factotum. He accompanied Haydn on his second journey to London, and tended him in his last years with the greatest care. Despite the proverb that 'no man is a hero to his valet,' Haydn was to Elssler a constant subject of veneration, which he carried so far that when he thought himself unobserved he would stop with the censer before his master's portrait as if it were the altar. Elssler copied a large amount of Haydn's music, partly in score, partly in separate parts, much of which is now treasured as the autograph of Haydn, though the handwritings of the two are essentially different. He survived his master thirty-four years, and died at Vienna, June 12th, 1843, in the enjoyment of 6000 florins which Haydn bequeathed to him as 'a true and honest servant.'"

concerts took place on Monday evenings, and were supported by an array of musical talent, which proves that London contained then, as it does now, the most generously appreciative, if not the most finely discriminating musical public in Europe. Besides the six new symphonies by Haydn which had been stipulated for, his former set were repeated, and some new quartets were also produced. At a rehearsal of one of the concerts, young Smart (afterwards Sir George Smart) was among the violinists in the orchestra. The drum-player failing to appear, Haydn called out from his seat at the piano, "Can any one here play the drum?" "I can," promptly answered Smart, who had never handled a drumstick in his life, and he took his place at the instrument, believing that all that was wanted was to count the bars and hit the drum at the right time, hard or soft. After the first movement Haydn called him down, praised his good intention, but sarcastically remarked that in Germany they had a way of stopping the vibrations of the drum after each note, which added to the good effect of it in the orchestra. He then took the drumstick and showed how it was done (remembering, perhaps, his own early experiment on Cousin Frankh's meal-tub). "All right!" remarked Smart, with unmoved self-possession; "if you like it better, I have no doubt we can do it that way in England, too."

An event of some interest in musical history was the appearance of Haydn and W. Cramer at the same concert, Cramer as leader of the orchestra, Haydn conducting from the pianoforte. During the summer of 1794, Prince Nicolaus Esterhazy, who was then travelling in Italy, took occasion to inform Haydn that he intended to reconstitute his Capelle, and to ask whether he wished still to consider himself as its head. Haydn promptly and gladly replied in the affirmative, and declared that as soon as his engagements in London were fulfilled, he should place his talent at the absolute disposal of the prince, whose faithful servant he had never ceased to be.

On the 26th of August Haydn paid a visit to Waverley Abbey, as the guest of Sir Charles Rich, and appears to have indulged in some gloomy reflections on the existence of the Protestant heresy, which had reduced to ruins what had once been a stronghold of his own religion. In September he went to Bath with Dr. Burney, on a visit to the celebrated singer, Rauzzini, who resided there. We can well believe that the three days spent in the then most fashionable watering-place in England with two such congenial companions, were among the pleasantest of Haydn's stay in England. We fancy we can see the trio, differing so widely in nationality and temperament, but united in sympathy for that art whose language, as Haydn said, was common to all the world, seated in an arbour in Rauzzini's garden, where Haydn has just inspected the memorial tablet erected by the singer over the grave of "his best friend." "*Turk was a faithful dog, and not a man,*" runs the inscription, and Haydn pulls out paper and pencil, and then and there turns the words into a four-part canon, treasured no doubt ever after by Rauzzini as a fitting tribute to the memory of his departed favourite. All the musical talent in London fled to Bath as soon as the season was over. Mara and Braham among vocalists, Giornovichj and Yaniewicz as violinists, Ashe the flautist, Mrs. Miles the pianoforte-player, all renewed their triumphs in the Pump-room at Bath, and there Haydn was lionized to his heart's content. But the three days were soon over, and at the beginning of October he was in London again for the winter season. This was an exceptionally brilliant one, and Salomon's new undertaking, the opera concerts, given in the new concert-room of the King's Theatre, was supported by an array of talent such as London had never before seen collected at one time. The first concert was given on February 2nd, 1795, and they were continued every Monday evening up to the month of May. The music was chiefly operatic, but one or sometimes two of Haydn's symphonies formed a regular item in the programme, the "Surprise" being always a special favourite.

These and other concerts at which he directed ("sass am Clavier," as he always expresses it in his diary), together with visiting and short excursions from town, filled the remainder of Haydn's last season in London. His last benefit concert was given on May 4th, and he expressed great satisfaction at its pecuniary result. "It is only in England," he says, "that one can make 4000 gulden (about 400*l*.) in one evening." His last appearance before an English audience was at the second of two extra opera concerts, given by Salomon on the 21st May and the 1st June. There can be no doubt that the success of the concerts was mainly owing to the popularity of Haydn's name and compositions. Salomon was able to continue them until 1799, when the undertaking died a natural death, one of Haydn's symphonies being an invariable feature of the programme until the very end.

During the latter part of his second visit to London, Haydn received many marks of favour from the royal family, and especially from the Prince and Princess of Wales. To be well received at Carlton House, and to be summoned to take part in the concerts given in the music-room, which Horace Walpole describes as the "jewel of all" the sumptuously appointed palace, was then the *ultima Thule* of the desires of every musician in England. The prince's taste for music was genuine and intelligent. He played the violoncello, and took his place in the orchestra, where his brothers, the Dukes of Gloucester and Cumberland, played the violin and viola. The evening concerts at Carlton House were given with a considerable degree of state, and the soloists were the best of the day. They were always ready to obey the prince's summons, although the payment for their services was often long delayed, sometimes forgotten altogether. Haydn himself, after waiting many months, at last sent in from Vienna a bill for 100 guineas for twenty-six attendances at Carlton House, a moderate enough demand, which, it must be added, was discharged at once. Beethoven, at a later time, was less fortunate. His "Battle of Vittoria," which he dedicated to the Prince Regent, was never paid for, nor was the receipt of it by the prince even acknowledged. At one of the prince's musical parties, which took place shortly after his marriage, the princess sang with Haydn and played a pianoforte concerto "fairly well," he says. The king and queen also admitted Haydn to a share of the favour which they had hitherto reserved exclusively for Handel. He was frequently invited to Buckingham Palace, and found some difficulty in refusing without offence the pressing invitation of the queen to remain and settle in England. But, indeed, the time of his final departure was very near. Prince Esterhazy was impatiently awaiting the conclusion of those engagements, which had been the only excuse alleged by Haydn for postponing the resumption of his duties as Capellmeister, and the master himself was beginning to feel the need of the quiet regularity of his home life. His last work for an English audience remains unfinished. It was a cantata for English words, Medham's "Invocation to Neptune," poor stuff, and not sufficiently inspiring to carry the composer on to the end. The only two numbers finished, a bass solo and a four-part chorus, are in the British Museum. Haydn received many presents from private and public friends before leaving England. These he valued exceedingly, and was fond of displaying them to his visitors in Vienna, and telling the anecdotes attached to each. One of the most original souvenirs followed him to Vienna from William Gardiner, a Leicester manufacturer and great lover of music (author of "Music and Friends, or Pleasant Recollections of a Dilettante," London, 1838), who sent Haydn, through Salomon, a complimentary letter accompanied by six pairs of stockings, into which were woven airs from Haydn's compositions, "Gott erhalte," the "Surprise" Andante, &c. Another curious gift was that of a talking parrot, which was sold for 1400 florins after its master's death. Haydn left London on the 15th of August, 1795. Independently of the lasting fame as a composer and the increased popularity with the English public which were the result of his second visit, he had made by his concerts, lessons, and symphonies (without counting his other compositions) about 1200*l.*, a sum sufficient to place a man so moderate in his wants beyond the reach of any anxiety as to the future. He travelled this time by way of Hamburg, Berlin, and Dresden, and was warmly received everywhere. On his arrival in Vienna he took up his temporary residence in the Neumarkt (now No. 2), probably because the alterations to his own house were still unfinished. In January, 1797, however, he removed to Gumpendorf, and there remained until his death, visiting Eisenstadt only during the summer and autumn. He never neglected his duties as Capellmeister, although the more menial of them were doubtless now performed by subordinates. The prince's birthday and other family festivities were always duly honoured by a specially composed mass or symphony, and the long list of Haydn's compositions between 1796 and 1803 proves that his right hand had lost none of its cunning. Indeed, the great work by which he is perhaps chiefly known to the world in general, was still to come. But before proceeding to an account of the "Creation" and the "Seasons," we must say a word on one of the best known of Haydn's songs, and his own favourite work. While in England he had always greatly admired our National Anthem, and regretted that his fellow-countrymen had no such inspiring expression for their feelings of fidelity to their sovereign. The war with France and the loyalty it evoked, intensified his regret and quickened his genius. Consultation with his friend Freiherr van Swieten led to the latter's suggesting the idea to the Austrian Prime Minister, Count von Saurau, who commissioned the poet Hauschka to provide Haydn with the words of a national anthem.

In January 1797, Haydn composed "Gott erhalte Franz den Kaiser," known to us as the Emperor's Hymn. The air is sublime and simple enough to be truly national, and so it has become. The devotional spirit displayed in Haydn's service, both to his emperor and to his own prince, is here faithfully reflected and the air is, as our readers know, in use in all our churches as a hymn tune. Haydn afterwards introduced a set of beautiful variations on it as the andante to the "Kaiserquartett" (No. 77).

He was very fond of playing it himself on the clavier when alone in his room, and on one of the last days of his life, when too weak to stand, he had himself carried across the room to the instrument, and solemnly played the hymn three times. It was his farewell to his art, his last expression of devotion and faithful service.

CHAPTER VIII.

THE "CREATION"—THE "SEASONS"—HAYDN'S LAST YEARS
—CONCLUSION.

HANDEL composed the "Messiah" in twenty-four days. The "Creation" occupied Haydn during eighteen months. Yet it can hardly be said that the latter composer was less rapid or spontaneous than the former. The truth is, that what in Handel was the natural and most fitting expression of his genius was in Haydn an effort suggested and urged upon him by others, not a work coming straight from his heart because it was "in him," like his quartets and symphonies. We do not hesitate to say that if the "Creation" had been written at the beginning of Haydn's career, instead of the end, had it been the work of an unknown composer, instead of that of a veteran whose fame was too firmly established to be shaken, it would certainly not have had the enthusiastic reception which was accorded it as the child of the old age of the great Haydn. As it is, its popularity, though brilliant, has been less solid and less lasting than that of his other works, and few of those whose knowledge of Haydn is confined to the fact that he was the author of the "Creation" would care to sit out a performance of the oratorio, which we seldom now see included in the repertory of choral societies. Even among his contemporaries there were not wanting good judges like Schiller, who called the "Creation" "a meaningless hotch-potch," or Beethoven, who made merry over its imitation of beasts and birds, but did the same in his "Pastoral" Symphony.

It would lead us too far, and be a transgression of the rule we have followed throughout this sketch of discussing

Haydn's works only so far as they had a bearing on his life, if we were to enter upon the much-debated question of programme music in general, and the extent to which it is justifiable or admissible. We need only say that those parts of the "Creation" which we still admire, and shall admire as long as music has the power of rousing the emotions and elevating the spirit of mankind, are not those which faithfully imitate natural sounds or strive to depict concrete ideas, but those which serve only to *suggest* the dawn of light, the rejoicing of the sun to run his course, the peaceful wandering of the moon across the heavens, the stormy upheaval of the ocean, or the first rush of the stream down the mountainside.

The idea of composing a great oratorio as the crown of his life's work was first suggested to Haydn by Salomon, who showed him a poem compiled for the purpose from Genesis and "Paradise Lost" by Lidley. Haydn took the book back with him to Vienna, and when his ardent admirer, the great musical connoisseur and friend of Mozart, Freiherr van Swieten, echoed Salomon's suggestion, showed it to him and asked him to translate and adapt it for the purpose. This Van Swieten rapidly undertook; he translated the poem into German with many alterations, and exerted himself to raise a guarantee fund among the Viennese nobility, in order to pay Haydn for the work. The ardour and religious spirit with which Haydn entered upon his task have already been alluded to (p. 41). "Never was I so pious," he says, "as when composing the 'Creation.' I knelt down every day, and prayed to God to strengthen me for my work." His anxiety and nervousness during the first performance of the oratorio show how earnestly he had set his heart on excelling in this branch of composition. "One moment," he says, "I was as cold as ice, the next I seemed on fire: more than once I thought I should have a fit."

The first performance of the "Creation" was given in Prince Schwarzenberg's palace by his private orchestra. The entire proceeds (350*l.*) were handed over to Haydn.

The success of the work was undoubted, and the audience was moved to genuine emotion. It was first publicly performed in Vienna on the 19th of March, 1799. After that it was given everywhere and became the rage, choral societies being formed for the purpose of studying it, and foreign capitals vying with Vienna in their homage to the work and its composer. Salomon at first threatened Haydn with an action for pirating his text, but self-interest speedily overcame his resentment, and we next find him writing for a copy of the score to be sent to him with all possible speed, in order that he may produce the work in London. Ashley, however, at that time conductor of the oratorios given in Covent Garden Theatre, was before him, and gave the first performance of the "Creation" on the 2nd of March, 1800. Salomon followed on the 21st of April in the King's Theatre concert-room, with Mara and Dussek in the principal parts. From that time until about five-and-twenty years ago, the "Creation" held its own with the "Messiah" and "Israel in Egypt" in the favour of the English public. In Paris the work was received with enthusiasm, a fact of which Haydn received a flattering proof in August, 1801, in the form of a gold medal struck in his honour after the design of the celebrated engraver Gateaux, bearing on the face a very tolerable likeness of Haydn, and on the reverse a lyre of ancient form, surrounded by a crown of stars. The inscription ran: "*Hommage à Haydn par les Musiciens qui ont exécuté l'oratorio de la Création du Monde au Théâtre des Arts l'an IX. de la République Française ou MDCCC.*" The medal was accompanied by a long complimentary address. Similar honours were showered upon Haydn during his later years, and it was evident from the pride he took in displaying to his visitors the medals that had been struck, and the poems that had been written in his honour, that they afforded him great gratification. His was a harmless and innocent vanity, showing itself neither in his works nor in his life, which was almost idyllic in its simplicity and absence of egotistical display.

Encouraged by the success of the "Creation," Van

I

Swieten persuaded Haydn to a second effort in the same direction, and this time furnished him with a text adapted from Thomson's "Seasons." The task was against the grain, however, and the work, although it retains much of the freshness and vigour which we are accustomed to associate with the very name of Haydn, bears evident signs of mental effort and fatigue. The subject was not congenial, and some of the words were so unsuited to music that he and Van Swieten very nearly came to a quarrel over them. The Emperor Francis once asked Haydn which of the two oratorios he himself preferred. "The 'Creation,'" answered Haydn. "And why?" "Because in the 'Creation' angels speak, and their talk is of God. In the 'Seasons' no one higher speaks than Farmer Simon." The oratorio, however, was enthusiastically received. Like the "Creation," it was first produced at the Schwarzenberg Palace; but public performances soon followed, and its success added considerably to Haydn's fame and to his fortune. The effort, however, was too much for him. An illness followed which left him an old man, pathetically conscious of his failing powers, and unwillingly relinquishing the active and industrious habits of his long and useful life. For the details of his last years we are mainly indebted to the landscape painter Dies, who sought his acquaintance through the sculptor Grassi for the express purpose of collecting from the veteran musician's own mouth materials for the biographical sketch which was published immediately after his death. Dies paid Haydn frequent visits in his little house at Gumpendorf, and encouraged the old man to forget his weakness and pain in recounting the triumphs and labours of his past life, and more particularly of his two visits to London, on which he always dwelt with peculiar pleasure. Our readers will pardon us for extracting a page from Dies's little book as the readiest and most interesting means of setting before them the musician and his biographer. The book is written in diary form, the entry which follows being dated August 17th, 1806 :—

"The long-continued heat of the weather had caused

this visit to be somewhat delayed. I found Haydn weaker than I had expected. His once gleaming eye was dull and heavy, his complexion sallow, and he complained of headache, deafness, forgetfulness, and other pains. I hid my concern with some difficulty, and sought for a cheerful subject of conversation. Where better could I find it for Haydn than in music? I succeeded happily in dispersing the cloud from his brow, and in answer to my question, 'How long is it since you touched the piano?' he seated himself at the instrument, began to improvise slowly and with difficulty, made a mistake, looked back at me, tried to repair his error, and in so doing made another. 'Ah!' he exclaimed after about a minute, 'you see it is all over with me! Eight years ago it was different, but the " Seasons " brought on this weakness. I ought never to have undertaken that work. It gave me the finishing stroke!' Haydn then stood up, and we walked slowly up and down the room. A heavy melancholy settled again on his brow, unrelieved by any passing ray of cheerfulness. 'My remaining days must all be spent in this lonely fashion,' said he. 'That should not be; you should always have a friend with you to cheer and amuse you.' 'But even that tires me. I have many visitors, but it confuses me so much to talk to them that at last I scarcely know what I am saying, and only long to be left in peace.'"

On his next visit, some months later, Dies found Haydn much stronger and more cheerful, and eagerly ready to tell him how a kind letter from Prince Esterhazy, promising him, at the instigation of the princess, an increase of salary, and giving him warm assurance of the prince's undiminished esteem and affection, had done him more good than all the doctors' stuff in the world.

Haydn composed very little after the "Seasons." Among his last works are several vocal quartets on which he set great store. They are chiefly of a devotional character, showing the direction in which his thoughts were turning. From one of these, "Der Greis," he took the first two lines, "*Hin ist alle meine Kraft, Alt und schwach bin ich,*" and used them as a finale to an unfinished quartet, of which the first two movements had been composed some years before. "It is my last child," said he, as he handed the quartet over to Griesinger's future custody; "but I think it is not unlike me." Haydn afterwards had the same passage printed as a visiting-card, in answer to the inquiries of friends.

In 1802 and 1803 he harmonized and arranged a number of Scotch songs for the publisher Whyte of Edinburgh, a work in which he took great pleasure, as likely to preserve his memory in Scotland. He also arranged some Welsh and Irish airs.

As long as he was able to rise from his bed at all, Haydn's daily routine continued as regular and frugal as we have seen it to have been throughout his life. He rose at half-past six or seven, shaved and dressed for the day at once; sometimes, before old age finally settled upon him, giving a lesson to a favourite pupil while these operations were proceeding. At eight he breakfasted, and the rest of the day was spent, according to his state of health, either in complete seclusion, or in receiving the visits of his friends, in improvising at the pianoforte, and in more or less successful attempts to apply himself to composition. He dined at two, supped sparely at ten, and retired to rest between eleven and twelve.

Once more, and for the last time, after several years of seclusion, Haydn appeared in public, and the occasion is a sufficiently memorable one to be narrated in some detail. On the 27th of March, 1808, the Society of Amateurs in Vienna gave as their last concert for the season a performance of Haydn's "Creation," with Carpani's Italian text. The composer received a pressing invitation to be present, and his health being better than usual he felt himself able to undergo the fatigue, particularly as Prince Esterhazy sent his carriage to conduct him to and from the hall of the University, where the concert was given. Haydn's entrance was announced by a burst of trumpets and drums and by the loud cheers of the audience. He was carried to an arm-chair placed in front of the orchestra, next to the seat occupied by Princess Esterhazy. Here he found himself surrounded by his most distinguished artist friends and pupils, and by nobles and ladies, who all received him with every mark of honour and esteem. Salieri conducted what all acknowledged to be an excellent performance. At the burst of music which accompanies the words, "And there was light!" the audience could no longer contain their enthusiasm, and applauded long and vehemently. Haydn, much overcome, pointed upwards and exclaimed, "It came from thence!" His excitement became so great that it was thought well to take him home at the conclusion of the first part. As he was carried out, his friends flocked round to take leave of him, among them Beethoven, who stooped to kiss his hands and forehead. At the door he bade his bearers pause and turn towards the orchestra. Then, lifting his hands as if in the act of blessing, he took his last, long farewell of his beloved " children " and of his still more beloved art.

Haydn's peaceful life was destined to end in the midst of war and war's alarms. Twice, in 1805 and 1809, he saw Vienna occupied by the French invaders. The trial was too much for his loyalty and for his personal devotion to his emperor and his prince. " This miserable war has cast me down to the very ground!" he would often say with tears, and no consolation that his friends could offer him' sufficed to soften the blow. In 1809 the city was bombarded, and a cannon-ball fell close to Haydn's dwelling. His servants were assisting him to rise and dress, and seeing their alarm to be greater than his own, he collected all his strength and exclaimed in a loud and firm voice,

"Do not be afraid, children! no harm can happen to you while Haydn is here." Overcome by the effort, he fell into a violent fit of trembling, which left him weaker than before, and it soon became evident to those around him that the master's days were numbered. The last visit he received was on May 17th from a French officer, who sang "In Native Worth" to him with so much expression that Haydn was deeply moved, and embraced him warmly at parting. The fact is significant, as proving once more that art has no enmities, and that music speaks that language of the heart which, as Haydn himself said, "is common to all the world." On the 26th of May he called his servants round him and was carried from his bed to the pianoforte. He then solemnly played the Emperor's Hymn three times over, and bade them lay him down again. He scarcely spoke after, and in five days, at about midnight on the 31st of May, 1809, quietly breathed his last. He was buried in the Hundsthurm Churchyard, close to the suburb where he lived, but as soon as peace was restored and the French had left Austria, his remains were removed by Prince Esterhazy and solemnly re-interred in the parish church of Eisenstadt. When the coffin was opened for identification before removal, the skull was found to be missing; it had been stolen two days after the funeral. A skull was afterwards sent to the prince anonymously as Haydn's, and was buried with his other remains; but it is a well-known fact that the real one was retained, and is now in the possession of the family of a physician in Vienna.[1]

On the 15th of June, Mozart's Requiem was performed in Haydn's honour at the Schottenkirche. Many French officers were among the mourners, and the guard of honour was chiefly composed of French soldiers.

Haydn had made arrangements in 1807 that upon his death all his books, music, manuscripts, and medals should become the property of the Esterhazys. Among the most interesting of the relics were twenty-four canons, the majority on German popular songs, which hung,

---

[1] Grove's "Dictionary of Music," vol. i. p. 716.

framed and glazed, in Haydn's bedroom. "I was not rich enough," he said, "to buy good pictures, so I have provided myself with hangings of a kind that few possess." His wife was once complaining of want of means, and wound up by saying that if he were to die to-morrow there was not enough money in the house to bury him. "In case such a calamity should occur," answered Haydn, "take those canons to the music publisher; I will answer for it, they will bring enough to pay for a decent funeral."

Haydn's will makes thoughtful provision not only for his poor relations, but also for his faithful and attached servants, Anna Kremnitzer and Johann Elssler. It contains bequests to various friends and patrons, and provides for the maintenance of the two poorest orphans of his birthplace, Rohrau.

Our task will have been undertaken in vain if it is necessary to conclude it with any remarks on Haydn's mental and moral characteristics, or on the place to be assigned to him in the history of music. Our object throughout the preceding sketch has been to present him to our readers as he appeared to his contemporaries and as he was, and to indicate his position in relation to his art from the larger and wider point of view which the rapid progress of music during the last century enables us to occupy. The greatest step of all, perhaps, in this progress was that taken by Haydn himself; his name and his labours omitted from any work professing to deal with the history of music would leave a gulf not by any means to be bridged over, and though one is tired of repeating the hackneyed phrase which hails him as "the creator of instrumental music," there seems no other which so fitly describes his life's work. Valuable as was his influence on composers of his own and succeeding times, however, Haydn did something more than found a school or develop a branch of his art. He brought music home to the hearts and minds of the people. He opened, not only to the musician and the connoisseur, but to all who have ears to hear, and hearts to be touched, a spring of the purest and most elevating pleasure. He left the world the happier and the better for his work in it. What can a man do more with the genius that heaven has bestowed on him? Music before Haydn's day was in danger of becoming inextricably entangled in the toils of pedantry and formalism. He boldly declared by his works that rules were made for the musician, not the musician for rules, and he might have adopted as his own Condillac's maxim: "Les règles sont comme des garde-fous mis sur les ponts, non pas pour faire marcher les voyageurs, mais pour les empêcher de tomber."

LIST OF HAYDN'S COMPOSITIONS, INSTRUMENTAL AND VOCAL.

I.

INSTRUMENTAL.[1]

125 Symphonies, including overtures to operas and plays.
Principal symphonies known by titles, with the approximate dates of publication.

Le Matin (D major), Le Midi (C major), Le Soir (G major), 1761.
The Farewell (A major), 1772 (letter B. in Philharmonic Catalogue).
Maria Theresa (C major), 1773.
Feuer Symphonie (probably overture to Die Feuersbrunst, A major), 1774.
La Chasse (D major), 1780.
Toy Symphony (C major), 1780.
La Reine de France (B major), 1786, for Paris.
The Oxford (G major), 1788 (letter Q. in Philharmonic Catalogue).
The Surprise, No. 3 of Salomon set (G major), London, 1791.
The Clock, No. 11 of Salomon set (D minor), 1794.
The Military, No. 12 of Salomon set (G major), 1794.

"The Seven Words from the Cross" (originally for orchestra,

---

[1] The difficulties in the way of compiling a complete and authentic list of Haydn's instrumental works are very great. Breitkopf's catalogue includes among the symphonies many works also to be found among the smaller compositions (Scherzi, Divertimenti, &c.), and others (owing to a transposition of the movements) are catalogued twice over. Haydn himself, in compiling his thematic catalogue, fell into the same error, and owned to considerable difficulty in deciding on the genuineness of some of the earlier instrumental pieces.

LIST OF HAYDN'S COMPOSITIONS.

afterwards arranged for two violins, viola, and bass, then for soli, chorus, and orchestra).

66 various compositions for wind and strings, separately or combined, including divertimenti, cassationi, &c.

7 Notturnos for the lyre or serenades.

7 Marches.

6 Scherzandos.

1 Sestet.

Several Quintets.

1 "Echo" for 4 violins and 2 cellos.

Feld-partien for wind instruments and arrangements from baryton pieces.

12 Collections of minuets and allemands.

31 Concertos—9 violin, 6 cello, 1 double bass, 5 lyre, 3 baryton, 2 flute, 3 horn, 1 for 2 horns, 1 clarino.

175 Baryton pieces. Arrangements of several of these were published in three parts, with violin (or flute), viola or cello as principal.

1 Duet for two lutes.

2 Trios for lute, violin, and cello.

1 Sonata for harp, with flute and bass.

Several pieces for a musical clock.

A solo for harmonica.

6 Duets for violin solo, with viola accompaniments.

30 Trios—20 for 2 violins and bass, 1 for violin solo, viola, and bass, 2 for flute, violin, and bass, 3 for 3 flutes, 1 for corno di caccia, violin, and cello.

77 Quartets for 2 violins, viola, and cello. The first 18 were published in 3 series, the next is in MS., then one printed separately, 54 in 9 series of 6 nos. each, 2 more, and the last.

CLAVIER MUSIC.

20 Concertos and divertimenti. One concerto is with principal violin; two only, G and D, have been printed; the last alone survives.

38 Trios—35 with violin and cello, 3 with flute and cello. Only 31 are printed.

53 Sonatas and divertimenti. Only 35 are printed; the one in C, containing the adagio in F, included in all the collections of smaller pieces, only in London.

4 Sonatas for clavier and violin. Eight are published, but 4 of these are arrangements.

9 Smaller pieces (including variations, adagios, and "différentes petites pièces").

1 Duet (variations).

II.

VOCAL.

Church Music.

14 Masses.
1 Stabat Mater.
2 Te Deums.
13 Offertories and 4 motets. Ten of the thirteen are taken from other compositions, with Latin text added.
1 Tantum ergo.
4 Salve Reginas and 1 Regina Cœli.
2 Ave Reginas; Responsoria de Venerabili.
1 Cantilena pro Adventu (German words).
6 Sacred arias.
2 Duets.

Oratorios and Cantatas.

"The Creation," "The Seasons," "Il Ritorno di Tobia," "The Seven Words," "Invocation of Neptune," "Applausus Musicus" (1768), Cantata for the birthday of Prince Nicolaus (1763), "Die Erwählung eines Kapellmeisters" (a cantata).

Operas.

"Der neue krumme Teufel," German opera or Singspiel.
5 Marionette Operas.
Italian Operas:—"La Canterina," 1769; "L'Incontro Improvviso," 1776; "Lo Speciale," 1768; "Le Pescatrici," 1780; "Il Mondo della Luna," 1777; "L'Isola Disabitata," 1779; "Armida," 1782; "L'Infedeltà Delusa," 1773; "La Fedeltà Premiata," 1780; "La Vera Costanza," 1786; "Acide e Galatea," 1762; "Orlando Paladino," 1782; "Orfeo," London, 1794.
Music for "Alfred," a tragedy, and various other plays.
22 Airs, mostly inserted in operas.
"Ariana a Naxos," cantata for single voice and pianoforte, 1790.
"Deutschlands Klage auf den Tod Friedrichs des Grossen," cantata for single voice with baryton accompaniment, 1787.
Songs:—12 German Lieder, 1782; 12 ditto, 1784; 12 single ones; 6 original canzonets (London, 1796); 6 ditto; "The Spirit Song," Shakespeare (F minor); "O Tuneful Voice" (E flat), composed for an English lady of position; 3 English songs in MS.; 2 duets; 3 3-part and 10 4-part songs; 3 choruses, MS.; 1 ditto from "Alfred;" The Austrian National Anthem, for single voice and in 4 parts; 42 canons in 2 and more parts;

2 ditto; "The Ten Commandments," set to canons; the same with different words under the title "Die zehn Gesetze der Kunst;" a selection of original Scotch songs in 3 parts, with violin and bass accompaniments and symphonies, London, (Vol. I. contains 100, Vol. II. 100, Vol. III. 47,—Haydn's own catalogue mentions 364, some of which were published by Thomson and Whyte, of Edinburgh); a select collection of original Welsh airs in 3 parts.

For EU product safety concerns, contact us at Calle de José Abascal, 56–1°, 28003 Madrid, Spain or eugpsr@cambridge.org.

www.ingramcontent.com/pod-product-compliance
Ingram Content Group UK Ltd.
Pitfield, Milton Keynes, MK11 3LW, UK
UKHW012209030426
469672UK00010B/135